The History that Counts

Whickwithy

The history that counts

Published by Whickwithy
whickwithy@gmail.com

ISBN: 978-1-7348221-8-2

The History That Counts by Whickwithy

First published Summer 2023

Previous efforts:
Sentience
A Sentient Perspective
Beauty & Fiction
Millennium
Book 6
The Sentient Struggle For Transformation
This And That
The Bane of Mankind
Ten

A new quote:
"The empires of the future are empires of the mind"
-Winston Churchill

We struggle to achieve all but that which will make us whole.

Book Eleven

Imagine a race of sentient beings that haven't quite figured out how to become fully human.

They have a secret, you see. The two genders are utterly confused by the secret that no one understands or admits.

The two genders remain at cross purposes. They remain at each other's throat. All because the male gender didn't like admitting that the act of coitus was not up to snuff and it was the male's responsibility.

The male gender never realized that it is crucial and simple to learn to love.

They never realized they were only following the instincts that had always burdened an animal.

Instincts are overruled by thought. Men are thinking sentient beings. Men can learn to love and it starts in bed.

Missing in action

It's a fool's game to believe we can do no better than an animal when it comes to coitus.

Any man can succeed at unassisted *loving* coitus. We have been misled by the animal. The goal is not to last two or three minutes. The goal is to last as long as *she* desires. A man has not taken on the mantle of his sentience until he learns that he can make *loving* coitus. There is no clock on the event when humans do it.

I will put my usual disclaimer even though it annoys me no end. This does not mean that every man *or woman* wants coitus. This just frees up the heterosexual to act like a human.

It is not something available for $299 from your favorite huckster. It is part of being human. Without it, we remain an animal.

I was just wondering how much should be charged for saving our sanity?

Personally, I would like to see confident masculinity replace toxic masculinity. So, no charge in those forms that can be free.

Maybe the real difference in humanity is the difference between having the tools of sentience and actually using them.

Maybe the real difference is the difference between sentience and sapience. We are aware. We just have to put that awareness to use. Then we can begin becoming sapient.

Thresholds of understanding

Each of my books has been a collection of insights on life for the purpose of understanding love. In the absence of achieving the one goal that really counts, I pursued its full understanding.

Kinda weird how I got here and the route I had to take. I had to discover how to right the sexual debacle in order to understand love. In retrospect, it makes sense, actually. That was preceded by forty years of wondering what is wrong with humanity.

I can't imagine that I can do any better than this book. Of course, I've been saying that since *Millennium*, so I'll just say that, once the new insights end, I'll consider myself finished. This feels so finished. It may or may not need polishing. I think ten years of writing and rewriting eleven books will have to do. I really believe in rewrites. I just can't imagine doing it any longer without an editor. Since no one can comprehend that we are not yet human, there are no editors available.

I understand love. It took a lifetime to understand what was missing. It is a terribly confusing image we have concocted, so far. It's not a surprise that it took a lifetime.

I was just thinking of a list of what love is not. It is not surrender to another. It is not validating yourself in the eyes of another.

It is not settling for something less after a few relationships because you become convinced we are not worthy of more.

It is sharing *everything* with another being. The physical act of love needs to become an act of fulfillment. If we walk away from a relationship, it should be with our heads up, undismayed. It has to end for meaningful reasons. I'm not sure they need to end at all.

We keep sidestepping the fundamental issue. Unassisted coitus, in its current form, is not love. Because there seemed no resolution to the fundamental issue of lasting long enough to make it an act of love, we have acted like it doesn't matter.

We were wrong on both counts. There is resolution and it does matter.

Love's absence may be even easier to identify. It's absence, by definition, is the lack of honour, compassion, integrity, empathy, dignity, sympathy, and a host of other characteristics that affirm our identity as a human, sentient, emotionally balanced, stable race of beings. If you need a lens, the opposing characteristics are just as obvious but I don't desire to get into them. I've written about them plenty in the other books.

The awful characteristics that humanity so brazenly puts on display today are not necessitated by existence. They exist due to two circumstances. Firstly, we have the perspective of a sentient race, whether we like it or not. Secondly, we are aware that there can be more to coitus. In our denial of the latter, the former is betrayed. We are human. It is ridiculous to believe our heightened intellect and awareness could not overcome the reason the animal fails and do something about it.

We keep viewing existence from the viewpoint of an animal. And, it begins with coitus. It has been a difficult demon to put away. I have done that. Now, it only takes male gender taking life seriously and facing the demon that has held it in thrall since the beginning.

We have never accepted our sentient awareness. It is shown in our defeat at the hands of an animal's instincts when it comes to coitus. It is shown in our stupour.

We make shit up instead. Like the idea that those stupid instincts of an animal are sacred or some stupid shit like that.

Goals

I have attained my goal.

I'm kinda surprised. I've said before that these books are a journey but I never felt I had reached its destination. It was more like recovering from exhaustion after each book at the oasis of further understanding. I think I now have traversed its length. It doesn't mean the ten books need a lot of reading. The love is in the physical representation of love, not any book. Once humanity (not this or that individual) realizes it can love, then the books will have little value.

Sometimes I wonder if anyone understands when I refer to humanity as a single entity.

At this point, just to throw the train off the tracks, I have to mention reincarnation. Seriously, these are the types of subjects I have been contemplating for a lifetime.

To me, reincarnation has been the most interesting of the various suggestions for what happens after we die. So, it was worth a *lot* of consideration. The most obvious conclusion, that death is the end of everything, doesn't take a lot of contemplation.

As usual, I can see the two sides of the argument (I *am* Gemini, after all, just to throw the discussion even further off track).

One scenario is that life just plugs away, one step after another. Fated to be by previous events. The other is that there is some je ne sais quoi involved. Probably not for the dullards.

I can think of particular instances in life that could explain my drive to seek out the answers to human life for seventy years. Beneath it all, though, it feels like I had something driving me along the way from the beginning.

Whether it is just pokes and prods from fate or a driving will that supersedes the grave that could not accept our lies, delusions, and deceptions remains an open question.

I felt the confusion that everyone else feels. I just battened down the hatches for a lifetime as the lies we endure began to build up beyond tolerance. It was like I just couldn't think of anything else worth doing than exploring the riddle of our ruin. I sure wasn't about to participate in it, though I did enough of that to still feel burned. Yes, I am one smart s.o.b.

We have always considered that our problems were based in the realm of survival, so there we pursued them.

The problem has always been the problem of transformation into a sentient state. The tools that Nature provided are not enough if we don't apply them. The survival and success of the race of humanity is based on the loving application of a sentient, stable, well-balance viewpoint. A fully sentient race would not distrust itself.

For my lifetime of seventy years, I have always wanted to dazzle. Now, here I stand and find myself dazzled to the bone.

I think I found, maybe, the central reason that it has taken three millennia to get here. I had to cut all entanglements with humanity after half a century of life *and* still have access to humanity, its knowledge, its great thinkers.

The cutting of family ties was easy. The beating drum of 'honour thy parents' didn't hold any water for me. The rest of the ties were much easier to abandon. I only keep one person in my heart and I chose well.

The access to all of humanity and its massive knowledge base was due to the internet, of course. Learned a lot there.

I can't say that humanity's antics disgusted me. We are not human yet and the behaviour should be expected from an animal with too much smarts and virtually no development of the heart.

Summation of ten

This is a summary of ten books and a decade long investigation, preceded by forty years of pondering what is wrong with humanity? Why have we been stuck in this hellhole condition for three millennia? What did we get wrong? Where did we go wrong?

I will concentrate my efforts in this book on what we got wrong and, once we get it right, how does it free us from the lunacy that we have endured for three millennia?

For a prehuman sentient being, sanity is on just the other side of crazy.

It is crazy to convince ourselves that we have attained our humanity while all hell continues to break loose.

Nature gave us so many gifts <u>that have *not* been utilized</u>.

We need to get beyond the poor assumption that we are human. We are not yet.

I think one of the issues is that men do not want to hear it because they do not want to admit they are bad at coitus. We all are. You should be able to last as long as *she* pleases with ease. Until it is done with ease by the man, we will remain a race dumbfounded by its own stupour.

Read Details, if you have any doubt. It's on my website, as well as below, if you bought this book. We have been thinking about it like an animal. We accepted defeat before we ever got a true gauge of the situation. It is easy to do and so very important to our sanity as a sentient race. It's as easy as breathing once we completely defeat the animal's instincts and learn to do it for a better reason than any animal could ever imagine.

It's hard for me to keep in mind that this is a vast reorientation of the human race into a truly sentient being unleashed from the delusions and deceptions of the animal that preceded us.

Don' talk to me about the paltry remnants of love that some people scrabble together in the absence of its fullest expression. It is just an animal scraping up the bits of what should be a feast for a sentient being.

I know, words like 'feast' puts you on your guard. Whoever heard of a race that doesn't bear a burden of misery? Who ever heard of a race of beings that doesn't walk around with lies caught between its teeth because it has no respect for itself?

Pointers

Men will not be whole until they realize they can love a woman as a human male knows damn well they should be capable, in the most natural manner possible.

It's like a layer of angst scattered amongst everything we do. It has never crossed anyone's mind that a man can do better than an animal at the act of coitus. Not by minutes, either. It becomes much easier to understand once you get past the idea that there is any time limit - for a human male.

#1 The male of the human sentient race has been avoiding self-actualization ever since our ancient ancestors closed the door firmly on loving coitus. Our ancient ancestors did not have the information available to them to overcome the issue at the heart of becoming human. It was too many dots for them to connect together. We have followed that lead for three millennia. *They* couldn't even begin to comprehend. We can.

<u>Loving</u> coitus is the most complete portrayal of love. Rutting coitus undermines that love. Not only does loving coitus create new life. In its final form for a sentient race it fulfills the physical aspect of love by <u>sharing</u> *all* of the pleasure. Love is an advanced form of caring only available to human, sentient beings. How can we be loving while the most intimate form of a male-female relationships is not?

You can quibble that a female animal knows love because it cares for its children. It doesn't matter. Until the male learns to love we are lost.

That is not saying that coitus is the only form of love that can be obtained nor is it saying it is the only form of love that must exist. It is only saying that, without loving coitus, we remain a mad animal because it prevents the male human from self-actualizing into a sentient state. Stable emotions and the intimate male-female *sentient* relationship suffers as long as it is remains incomplete *from a sentient perspective.* The expansion of caring into the loving portrayal of life that only a sentient being can conceive is based on sharing of the most transcendental physical experience in life. It is not shared until both achieve orgasm. The crucial form of that physical sharing that makes babies is required. Coitus' embellishment into a loving event is all human and we are not human until it is so.

Men can overcome the instincts of the animal that makes it all end way too soon to be called love.

The lack makes a mockery of our sentient state. Somewhere deep inside, men know that they should be able to do better. It confounds them from the time they reach puberty and continues to do so for the rest of their lives. It is not a matter of moving the threshold from a few seconds to two minutes, but by removing the threshold entirely. The threshold that counts, the threshold that every man desires, the threshold that makes us human is lasting as long as *she desires and deserves.*

Men will always remain mad (on a sliding scale; both definitions apply) until they realize they have been duped. They can make coitus a loving event with ease. The *male gender* must learn to make love. Not individuals here and there but the combined consciousness of the human male of the species must accept that they can love in the most intimate physical manner possible. Love is the most important form of human, sentient communications. It starts in bed. Without it, the rest of our communications remains gibberish.

#2 The male gender's achievement of self-actualization has been on hold for three millennia. All because our ancient ancestors were stopped cold when it comes to making coitus a loving event. They were stopped cold because the achievement of loving coitus takes a fully aware sentient mind to succeed. The most difficult success is realizing all of the nonsense that has been thrown in the way for millennia. The act of loving coitus itself is not difficult at all. It is only a few corrections to the instinctual actions that make the difference. I have uncovered that for you. You are welcome.

#3 For thee millennia, we have tried to act like sex is no big deal. That was the first lie, the misrepresentation of a sentient existence due to an animal's perspective remaining dominant. Just" get it done" is the cry of the most witless animals.

Then the lies continued to pile on. Coitus was just for making babies. It had no other use according to some religions. Sex is a curse on humanity. That was to compensate for the fact that women weren't getting anything out of the experience except disappointment. Since the species worries about its ongoing existence, we twisted the idea even further. Coitus was the *only* acceptable form of sex! Any way in which a human couple could achieve loving fulfillment for the woman was evil.

The wall of lies that has been erected has isolated us from our sentient awareness. Not purposely. It was done because the shame of failure of the male gender was too much for the simple minds of our ancient ancestors. They could not contend with their failure and no immediately apparent resolution was available.

Sex was a curse on humanity, so why should they be interested in it? I mean, duh. Can anyone think of a reason that people might be interested in sex, above and beyond bringing new life into existence? Like it's the most transcendent form of pleasure in existence? It is the *sharing* of that transcendent experience that makes all the difference in the world. It is not the orgasm that is that pleasure. It is the *sharing* of orgasm that is the ultimate pleasure. That represents love versus the physical pleasure alone that is the domain of the animal.

Or, as I like to say, men take, women give and it all starts in bed. That is not human. That is only the rendering of an animal's existence.

The lies just kept piling on. Women consciously realized, at some point, that they could also achieve that incredible sensation of climax.

So, we had a form of sex necessary for making babies: coitus, in which only one participant experienced the extraordinary pleasure of the transcendent pleasure. Then, there were all the others ways that could provide for the pleasure of both or, in conjunction with coitus (e.g. foreplay, cunnilingus, dildo, switching teams, etc).

Let's peer closely at a couple in which the woman says, "I love my man. I don't need no damn orgasm". It sounds real goo on paper but how often do you think the woman is going to be interested in only watching her partner achieve the transcendental state. If he's brutal enough, mean enough, he can get his way and have it often. Doesn't sound much like love to me.

The history that counts

We became sentient long ago. Sentience indicates that we are much more aware of what is going on around us than animals. That is a difference that counts. Until our awareness correlates all that we perceive with a sane representation of life, we will remain at a loss causing destruction willy-nilly.

One aspect of primate life was not satisfactory at all to our heightened awareness. Rutting, where only the male achieves orgasm, was found wanting. Men, of course, tried to change that ... and failed. *For three millennia.* All because it seemed impossible to the dim minds of our ancestors. They set the stage and their descendants followed the script. Many cursed sex and our sentient state. That is still true three millennia later. It could have driven the race crazy and ended us.

With the patience of a mountain, women said, "Okay, I get it. You guys haven't figured out how to make coitus a loving event yet. Take your time."

Unfortunately, men could not confront the problem for long without losing their minds and the race was far too unsophisticated to address the issue initially. The race learned to make excuses, as the generations rolled on without success. The uncanny thing is that no one really said a word about it for three millennia! Little hints but no one was willing to state outright that coitus was broken. Instead, just more excuses, more justifications for remaining no better than a demented animal. We quit trying to resolve the issue long, long ago. We buried the problem as deep in the weeds as we could. We declared three minutes a success because we continued to approach the problem like an animal: hold on for dear life and hope for the best.

The first step towards a sentient state is provided by the toolkit that Nature made available to a sentient race, both physically and mentally, a high intellect combined with very heightened awareness. That is sentience. The second is the realization and understanding of the tools provided by Nature and adapting them to work for a sentient species. That is self-actualization.

We have prevented our self-actualization in the case of loving coitus, by far the most important aspect of utilizing the tools that Nature provided for a sentient race, because we had blinded ourselves to the possibility. I will reiterate, since so many people are so touchy about an already touchy subject, this does not preclude any other form of physical love. The members of a *fully evolved* human race couldn't care less how any particular sentient being achieves love. The only requirement is that *all* forms of sentient physical love are available to choose from.

We self-actualize in a big way when the male gender realizes they can make coitus a loving event.

Men are not just animals. It seems impossible from an animal's perspective, which most men retain, because they follow the animal's instincts without fail. Men can easily overcome the instincts of an animal because we think.

It will be obvious, once the light dawns on humanity. It is dead easy. The most difficult hurdle is the wall we have built around sex and, especially, coitus. We treat it like the plague.

Make no mistake, if men thought there was a remote possibility they could perform to (their own) expectations, they would. They do not because they fear facing the failure as much as the human race fears talking about it. Now, they can fact it and succeed. You are welcome.

Women have put up with so much since the beginning. All because sex hit humanity right between the eyes. Men take, women give, and it begins in bed. It need not continue.

Humanity's self-actualization was stopped cold by our inability to realize that all it takes to attain loving coitus is understanding the workings of a human body and mind.

We become human when the male gender finally understands that it can overcome the instincts that usually cause it to be over in a hurry. It's not an option for a sentient race that wants to rid itself of its insanity. The animal cannot be tamed or trained but it can be transformed. Into a human.

We are not yet human, due to a single missing piece of the puzzle. The race has not yet self-actualized regarding the most important event between a couple. Without a stable foundation for the intimate relationship of a couple, how in the world do you think humanity can ever attain its sanity? The lack leaves the rest of our sentience in shambles.

I have resolved men's issue completely. This is not like a master class in karate. It is more like a master class in tiddlywinks. Anyone can learn it. You're welcome. It's on my site under "Details", as well as my last six books.

Some men have solved how. I also solved how it works. Not to mention that I also correlated the importance to our sanity as a sentient, self-aware race. Never send a physiologist or psychologist to solve a plumbing issue. Always send a polymath.

We are not self-aware until we admit the issue that has confounded us for millennia and realize it is amenable to the toolkit that Nature provided. You are at the doorstep.

As much as I've bitched about the three millennia it took to get us here, it's a drop in the bucket of time. It is now time to become human.

I really can't explain it any better than that.

Addendum: It's a good thing that a lot of people engage in coitus. It keeps humanity from going extinct. It is a bad thing that coitus does not reinforce the love between two people that our sentient state makes possible because there is seldom *sharing* of the *full* experience. It is really bad for the sentient experience that it causes bitter feelings for all that overwhelm any chance of clear thinking.

The physical act of sharing *everything* regarding the physical experience of love transforms the experience of life. It becomes human. It is not love until orgasm is shared.

It's no surprise that we are ashamed of the act of coitus. It is still the inept act of an animal, almost invariably.

Humanity will not attain its sentient state until the male gender realizes that it is more than an animal. The male gender can learn to love. Being sentient is about self-actualization. Men can and must learn to love.

So far, we have attained the state of a demented animal. We can attain an unobstructed sentient view of reality.

As long as men continue to sell themselves short when it comes to love, what else can be expected? For millennia, men have fought to prove their worth in the most insane ways beside the mounting awareness that they are not. It is time for men to self-actualize and comprehend that the act of love is within the purview of a sentient male. We won't be human until that happens.

It's not even difficult except for all of the baggage we have carried along with us. The act of loving coitus confirms our sentient state in so many ways. Love cannot be complete without it.

We have remained in a stupour for millennia because men could not comprehend that they are so much more than an animal. They took the word of their ancestors for three millennia. That's what my eleven books are all about. They explain the dizzyingly complex situation that has held us back for three millennia through delusions, deceits, and confusion.

As long is it remains the common belief of men that they can do no better, men will do no better. Worse yet is the still too common belief that the sexual gratification of their partner is of no importance. Hey, we're making babies, right? What else could be necessary?

I mean, duh. Wrong. We throw the whole of sentient reality into confusion as long as we don't admit the truth. Sentient beings are not animals and we have to admit it and prove it. We are aware of far more than any animal. Our realizations have to coincide with reality. Right now, our delusions are so averse to a sentient reality that it buries our humanity.

Details, which you can find on my blogspot website (sentienceww.blogspot.com) or in any of my last five books, explains what men have been missing for millennia.

Where do we go from here

I think one of the places that a sentient race will be able to explore with much more acuity is our desires.

Everything will get so much better because we will no longer need to lie about our desires.

The going thought is that men only desire their own fulfillment. Don't be naive. They *learn* to fulfill their own desires only because they fail to provide the fulfillment to their mate and their mates have mostly accepted it quietly for far too long 'for the good of the race'. There is no good in the lack of love.

There's no doubt. We desire love and have been frustrated in achieving it since we first conceived the term. It is the other desires that will take on a new light.

Think about it this way. Coitus is required for procreation. For an animal, it was never meant to be a fulfilling prospect. That's why the western churches concluded that sex is just for making babies. Sex was such an awful prospect that western churches concluded that their priests should not indulge. There's a plan for insanity. All of the ways in which we tried to get around the problem (e.g. foreplay) were fine, sort of a compromise with our sentience.

We became confused between what we wanted and what we needed. I've mentioned before how all of this is reflected in the songs we sing. My favorite example of this one is probably London Grammar's song on the subject. Hanna was dead right in her summation of wants and needs ... and it breaks us.

We need sexual release. For men, it is crazy important. For women, I couldn't say. They have learned to mask their feelings so well that I'm not even sure how many know what they really want. Men clearly haven't a clue what they really want - after the grinding experiences of failure post-pubescence - or bury their desires in utter disappointment.

One thing is clear: we want love. Every single one of us wants love. When it is denied (which is essentially *always* in our current conditions), it cannot flourish. It becomes deadened.

That is why older folks most often haven't much love left in their systems. This is a fine point that I have tried to stress. Love does not wither on the vine when it is not consummated but it is destroyed when it fails. In other words, in a world in which any man engaging with any woman succeeds at making it a loving event, those that do not find someone with whom to engage do not go crazy. They are supported by a human-wide culture of love.

They know love. They just have to find some other outlet for their sexual urges. Hopefully (and I believe it), it will most often take the form of physical love with another person.

It's not like I am closing any doors. I am only opening the one that provides balance and sanity. If, for instance, a couple chooses some other form of achieving the mutual pleasure of sex, it must not be because of the absence of the most natural form of physical love.

Most importantly, we need unfettered love to blossom into our sentient awareness.

Men will not be whole until they realize they can love a woman as a human male knows damn well they can in the most natural manner imaginable. Once that becomes the reality, love will flourish.

Humanity's Sanity

Humanity's sanity is attained when our sentient awareness correlates with all in our purview, when no major lies remain in our sentient perspective. One such awareness is to realize that mutual sexual pleasure is human. The awareness that floods our perspective with love is the self-respect and self-confidence that is achieved by making loving coitus as natural as being human.

Summary of Details

Does it surprise you, men, that you can do so much better at coitus than your ancestors that have remained so tightly coupled to the animal's way of thinking through cajolery and self-enforced delusions? The extent of our delusions are truly mind-boggling.

Below, I make two attempts to make it clear how and why a man can learn to last as long as *She*desires (excluding exhaustion). I am uncertain how to combine the two attempts.

As I have said, it is so simple that words will hardly be needed in the near future, once we get over the hurdle of the nonsense we have adopted for three millennia.

One generation free of the nonsense and we will be on our way. It is as easy as riding a bike or learning to walk. It is only the *mindset* of an animal that impedes our progress. Do not underestimate the damaging effects of that mindset.

It may take everything a man has to get over the hurdle of lies.

So, I will leave both attempts without trying to combine them. There is some repetition. You probably need it, at this point.

One-shots

Below, I get into the many details, but the resolution itself is simple to understand. Don't squeeze the sex glands in the crotch. It is much simpler than it sounds. An animal has no control over the muscles that squeeze the sex glands in the crotch, which begins the process of ejaculation. Because we think, we can. We are no longer just animals.

There is no reason for the sex glands to be squeezed during coitus other than inertia of the past. Well, like I said, the details are provided but I just wanted to give a few snapshots regarding the situation.

Another one-shot is that, as we mature into our sentience, older men, that did not learn the nuances in their youth, might find it more difficult to overcome the habits of failure and the muscles that have atrophied over a lifetime. It is not impossible. It just becomes more difficult and may take longer to succeed. I can personally attest to this. Building up muscles that have withered through misuse and learned all the wrong lessons, can recover. For a younger person, it should be easy, if they have not learned the wrong lessons.

It just takes a level of conscious awareness and understanding that is unavailable to an animal. We are not just an animal.

The Leap Never Taken

If any man had ever taken the time to think, he would have realized it is not *his* shame. It might be an animal's shame, but they are too witless to do anything about it, even if they are aware of the failure. Who knows?

For a human male, though, he has enough sense to *think*, if he is only willing, if his thought processes are not restrained by lies and conditioning. He is not witless, but he is very, very aware of his failure and does everything he can to avoid thinking about it. That is an understandable problem. Get over it.

Man has remained discombobulated by the inertia from the past. The hopelessness has been passed down to him, generation by generation, further distorting our sentient reality.

Everyone is convinced that a man is on some kind of a countdown clock, when it comes to sex. The clock starts ticking for an animal, but that does not need to be the case for a human male *unless he doesn't think things through.*

Every man has the evidence right in front of him that the clock can go into suspended animation. Any man worth his salt has, errrr, taken care of things for himself, on occasion (rather than having it happen at an embarrassing, inopportune moment).

Did you ever notice how difficult it is to even get the clock started in such a case? There are reasons for that and it hints at why that clock should be completely under the man's control. It is nothing more than an illusion for a sentient being.

One difference between the two events is that one cannot tickle themselves. It does *not* happen during 'rehearsals'. That is part of what makes skin on skin such a glorious event, unmatched by anything else in life. The erogenous zones, not to mention every nerve ending in your body goes into orbit with skin on skin action. Essentially, the coital act has elements similar to the two well-defined ticklish responses in other areas of the body. In this case, the erotic sensations, so similar to tickling, trigger the muscles in the crotch, *if a man continues to think like an animal*. That is critical.

There are other differences, as well. They all add up to a man being able to make love the way he has always dreamed *if he takes the time and effort to think it through.*

Another difference is that, when engaging a woman, there is movement that is usually missing when one 'rehearses'. The movement of the hips and crotch area. That movement, when studied, makes it clear what is happening, why the animal has *no* control *and* why every human (not just men) should, if we just quit shutting the whole conversation down.

An animal operates by instincts. Let me interpret "instincts" for you. It is muscle memory overriding conscious thought. Instincts can override the ability to think and, in the absence of conscious thought, cause something to be performed the way it has always been done.

Sound familiar? It should. It is the exact way in which we have treated coitus for millennia. Like a witless animal.

One mistake *the animal makes* should be glaringly obvious but, somehow, it rarely really hits home. There is a driving urge for a man to dive as deep as he can, especially once the cascade of ejaculation is sensed. It is often even encouraged by the woman. It is a really good feeling.

Unfortunately, it encourages the *approach of climax* for the man *in short order*. Save it for the grand finale. It will be the finale, whether it is grand or not. There is a certain depth that can be approached without encouraging climax for the man.

If you remain an animal, it is called rutting. It is done without thinking. It is *done* way too early for a human. Abandon all thought (and the woman in your arms) and proceed to please yourself.

The musculoskeletal structure is set up to begin the discharge process when you dive too deep and squeeze the sex glands in your crotch (located very near the bottom of your shaft).

In essence, it is all about the glands in the crotch that retain the vast majority of the fluids that make up the discharge of semen. When those glands are squeezed, Bang! You're done.

Even without the deep dive instinct, there is one more instinct that must be avoided. This one is a little more subtle and it is crucial.

The muscles in the crotch, surrounding the glands, when flexed and released, squeeze the glands in a couple of ways.

They do not need to flex and release. This will take a little more effort than "don't do that, find the limit" as is the case with the depth of your stroke. You will actually have to think it through.

There are two ways the squeezing action can happen. Both are nothing more than instincts of the animals that came before us that can be overcome easily - *if you can think like a human.* Animals perform those actions because they *can't* think. We perform them because we don't think.

Men don't think it through because they never realized it was nothing more than instincts. No one told them any different. Well, I'm telling you, DON'T.

The two actions? First of all, the muscles in the crotch are flexed during the movements of coitus *without thinking.* The muscles in the crotch *are not necessary for any movement.* That is not why those muscles are there. They are only flexed during bodily movement because we never think about it. All of the bodily movements can be accomplished without flexing the muscles in the crotch.

With just a little forethought and practice, a man can avoid using them during coitus - until it is time. The muscles in the legs, back, torso, etc can provide all movement *without* the use of the pelvic muscles (i.e. the muscles in your crotch).

It takes practice, of course, but the crotch muscles are independent of movement. You don't flex them because they are needed for movement. You flex them because of instincts. No one ever really thought about it because we were all acting like scared little children unwilling to look under the bed.

Secondly, the 'ticklish' (erogenous, if you prefer) response mentioned earlier. The muscles in the crotch get almost no exercise. Because of that, they do not respond properly to your commands.

While performing the particular movements of coitus, it is dangerously easy for those muscles to inadvertently and unnecessarily spasm in response to the mind-bending erotic 'ticklish sense'.

The skin on skin action is similar to tickling a person's feet with a feather or the more intense tickling reactions of the muscles under the arms. It is a challenge to avoid flexing those muscles due to this, but not impossible. The same holds true of the muscles in the crotch. Exercising those muscles is crucial and simple. It takes no more than a couple of minutes a day.

It is far from impossible. It's just something that no one has ever spent any time studying. So much for the 'mystery'.

It takes a *little* forethought and a *little* regular exercise of those muscles in one's crotch to be able to prevent the unwilling muscle contractions.

That's it. The exercise makes the muscles more supple. The forethought and practice make them responsive to your commands (including unresponsiveness to the ticklish reaction except as desired when the time is right). That's all there is to controlling those muscles and, thus, controlling ejaculation. So much for mystery.

In other words, yes, you can be human.

I came up with the terms, "don't twerk" (i.e. don't dive deep) until the lady sings (i.e. is ready for her own climax or climaxes) and "don't jerk" (i.e. don't flex those muscles in the crotch) to make the concepts easy to remember. I know, corny.

The second one, "don't jerk" is worth a little exploration. The two points during a stroke that are most dangerous for causing those pelvic muscles to inadvertently flex are the two endpoints of the stroke. Be careful when transitioning direction.

As I said, it is as easy as riding a bike, once you learn what needs to be done.

If you are not enraged by the fact that this has been there all along and, somehow, your ancestors never got a clue, don't feel alone. I was burned for a lifetime. I hope you catch on sooner. My fury, once I discovered the dodge game we have played, nearly consumed me.

As one learns what they are doing, unless the woman is doing her best to catch you off guard (which may become a great game to see who can outlast whom), it becomes easy to last as long as one desires. Can you imagine coitus as a loving, fun event?

There is, of course, a lot of fine print. It is no big deal. Only one more regarding early discharge. It's also the easiest to understand.

If the glands are overfull, nothing is going to stop them from being squeezed and, thus, beginning discharge. No different than the bladder being in the same condition.

The other fine print is the woman's anatomy. If you want to be her lover, if you want to make love to her, for the first time in your life; the first time in the long and painful history of humanity; if you want her to climax, you will also want to learn a little about her anatomy. I cover that, to some extent, in some of the other books, but I will mention the essentials.

The nub of the clitoris, the most erotic response zone on a woman is located *outside* and just above of the vagina. It should be easy to stimulate as long as you know where it is. It is usually a half-inch or less above the opening. So, it is all about positioning.

If you aren't paying attention, you may very well miss stimulating it at all. The rest of the clitoral erogenous zone? Within *an inch or so, just inside* the opening.

Why, then, is the deep dive so enticing for both the man and the woman? Ummm, it is an incredible feeling? *As is mutual orgasm* (not necessarily simultaneous, though that might make a nice goal). Save it for the grand finale. It's the icing on the cake for the humans that finally can make love.

All that is required for stimulating a woman is within an inch or two of the opening of the vagina. You should be able to go further without over-stimulating yourself, just be careful.

The other aspect that I will stress, I am certain will need no emphasis once we become human. A man is easily aroused. A woman, at least in our prehuman condition, not so much. Your efforts to arouse her need to be in everything you do. The way you touch her, the way you look at her. The way you communicate with her. In essence, the way you romance her. The way you love her.

I don't worry about this too much. It isn't that men can't conceive of what love means and how to achieve it. It is only unremitting failure to last long enough to count that has done men's character and existence in.

Romance is far more than the effort taken to get her in bed the first time. It is the effort that should last a lifetime amidst the incredible backdrop of love.

Oh, goodness! You will be able to spend a lifetime gazing into her eyes as she transcends this existence right along with you. I am so jealous! ... In a good way. ;~j

That was the latest attempt to explain. This is my old self raging, to some extent, at the stupourdity of the ages (that made me less than I could have been) along with a bit more analytical approach as it leads into Details.

Leading into Details

All of the books that I have written over the last twelve years are about the fact that men never learned to transform the act that creates life into an act that also creates love. That has resulted in damage to the human race's development as a sentient race.

The male *gender, not a few individuals*, needs to learn that men can learn to love - easily. It needs to become firmly implanted into the brain of the human species. In other words, the human consciousness must become certain of the fact.

Have you had "that talk" with your father yet? How did it go? Did he fumble around and never say anything of import? Was he utterly relieved when you told him, it's okay, dad, I know all about it. Which you didn't.

Don't hold it against him. I'm not sure any man has really known how to love a woman physically before. They've usually known what the animal passed on to us. Rut. Stick it in and get it over with. Maybe think about baseball. Some may have actually stumbled onto a way to last long enough. That is not the same as the human potential to completely understand the situation and overcome the limitations of the animal with full awareness.

I am all about simplifying what I am trying to say. Even so, it is just such a complicated picture - in that we have been taught wrong about essentially everything for three thousand years - It has taken me writing eleven books to understand thoroughly and explain. I am on my twelfth and final book.

We have made a mess of our sentient aware existence.

The easiest part to understand is how to love a woman physically in the most elegant manner possible. The loving and human version of coitus. It is the implications, obfuscations, and refutations regarding this uniquely human, sentient experience that has made the rest so complicated.

The saying goes that men want sex and women want love. That portrays the dilemma poorly. Men *settle* for sex, in utter frustration, because they have not been able to fulfill the act of love the way they have always desperately desired to do and Nature always intended to make a unique sentient experience.

This is about how a man learns he can last long enough to make coitus a loving, human, sentient, fulfilling event. This is all about how a man learns that he is not held hostage by an animal's instincts, low grade thinking, and a dim-witted brutish approach to life. This is all about how a man learns that he is not just an animal.

A man does not differentiate himself from an animal until he realizes that he can love. That is unique to humans and loving coitus bridges the gap. He doesn't learn to love fully until he can express that love in its physical form in the way Nature provided. Anything less is a disappointment. It is the only purely human sexual act. Eye to eye, celebrating life and love.

Early male humans equated themselves with animals and conducted themselves as such. They took a craven approach to life that has remained, in great part, to this day.

Today's male humans remain mystified by their failure. They have accepted it as such because that is how it has always been. The leap to see beyond the paradigms that broke our humanity are formidable. The act itself is simple.

I've learned a lot since the initial insight of "Don't twerk or jerk until the lady sings" and made it all available in most of the books starting with *Millennium* (my favorite).

Details

Number one. A man is not on a countdown clock in any way when it comes to coitus. Only animals are. That mistaken belief has stopped the male gender in its tracks for so long. The belief is that, once you are aroused and penetrate, the ejaculation process is off and running. That is true for an animal. It is not true of a human.

The huge mistake compounded by that belief is that the best you can do is hold on for dear life as you helplessly watch the tidal wave of ejaculate makes its way downstream. Let me be crystal clear. Any way in which you attempt hold back the tide, once begun, is bad. It can cause damage.

So, no, you are not on a clock and it is not a good idea to try to hold back the process of ejaculation, once begun in earnest. If you catch it early enough, you can stop all activity long enough for things to settle down. Some refer to this as edging. It works. Keep it in your toolbox for making love, but don't expect to use it except as you are learning to master your body. Forget master of the universe. Master of your body is far more fulfilling.

What really works is to understand why the process of ejaculation gets started and what can be done about it so that you become a master of your own body. It's not magic. You are only held back by the witless instincts of an animal that have never been investigated fully in any way before.

There is only one thing that gets the ejaculation process started. Squeezing the sex glands in the bottom of your crotch, your pelvic region. *That* begins the process. Nothing else.

What happens is that the glands gets squeezed by two events, the muscles and/or the musculoskeletal structure in the pelvic region. The squeezing can be avoided. They are squeezed due to following the instincts of an animal without even realizing it.

There is one condition in which there is no stopping it. It will not be stopped if the glands are overfull. It is already being squeezed by being overfull. The solution is obvious.

Otherwise, two primary instincts cause the beginning of the end. One is simple to understand and control. That is the effect of the musculoskeletal structure of the pelvic region. The other is overcome by mastering the muscles in the pelvic region of your body. It's not difficult to do. It was just difficult to unravel.

There is a desire to immediately plunge as deeply into that heavenly place, as you can. Save it for the grand finale. Doing so forces the musculoskeletal structure around the pelvic region into a position to squeeze the glands. It best to remain as shallow as possible until you learn what you are doing.

All of the woman's erotic nerve endings are within two inches or less of the opening, anyways. The erogenous zone with the most erotic nerve endings is the clitoral nub which is located about half an inch *outside* of the vagina. If you do no stimulate this clitoris button, it is unlikely you will be stimulating the woman enough to achieve own orgasm. More details later.

The one that is more difficult to comprehend is how the muscles in your crotch operate. The more I study it, the more convinced I become that within two or three generations, without all of the impediments that are currently thrown into our faces, like the bad habits acquired, the missing knowledge, and the expectation of failure, combined with a growing confidence by the male gender, will make it as easy as learning to ride a bike. It is a different effort.

You have to teach yourself to master those muscles and not use them. It is not difficult. It is just that we never tried because we always veer completely away from any thoughts on the matter due to the paralyzing fear of admitting failure.

The muscles in your crotch, your pelvic muscles, will squeeze the sex glands if flexed. *They don't need to.* Those muscles only contract because we never thought about it. We react like an animal without thought. Animals contract those muscles because they have the wit of, well, an animal.

The pelvic muscles have nothing to do with movement and, yet, during the movement of coital engagement, they contract and relax because we just don't think about it. We've never trained the muscles.

It's easy to prove. Try moving any part of your body by using only your pelvic muscles. You can't do it. They are not attached in that way. They are not muscles for moving. They are attached in a way that controls the output of bodily fluids. In the case of ejaculate, flexing the pelvic muscles, during tumescence, will start the process of ejaculation by squeezing the sex glands.

During coitus, you have to learn to move your body *without* contracting the pelvic muscles. It's not really a big deal, once you become familiar with the idea. It's not like trying to master the heart muscles (which also can be done to some extent; i guess some may even be able to stop the heart completely. it's just that you never hear about it because they are dead).

The pelvic muscles are not needed at all during coitus. It is just a matter of learning to move the body without allowing those muscles to flex. It may be helpful to use them when the woman says it's time to end it, but I am not even certain that it will ever be necessary. A deep dive is the best, most satisfying, and certain trigger. It is a nearly unavoidable trigger, which is why it is so commonly used before it is necessary.

This is why I came up with the phrase early on, "don't twerk or jerk until the lady sings." It's trite but it gets many points across. It points out, for instance, a most critical necessary point of control for the pelvic muscles. When changing directions, especially on the backstroke when you are withdrawing, it is *very* easy to let those muscles contract until well-trained. There is a tendency to jerk.

There is a third effect that needs to be considered but it is part of mastering the muscles, and not nearly as difficult. That is the erotic sensation. This is how the head of the penis gets involved. The erotic sensations that can blow your mind can also trigger a spasming contraction of those muscles.

In essence, it is no different than the tickling sensation in other parts of your body. You can master the spasming by exercising those muscles, making them more supple and responsive. Don't freak out. It should take more more than a couple of minutes a day to train them, maybe less for someone that matures into his sexuality already knowing what to do.

Those muscles, essentially, have never been consciously controlled or trained and made supple. In fact, you can control the muscles reaction to tickling in any part of the body, if necessary. (i had a cruel older sister. i know). You can control any tickling sensation. If anything, it makes the enhanced experience more mind-blowing.

Once you master those muscles, some intriguing possibilities begin to present themselves. As I mentioned, the erotic zones of the woman are all very close to the opening. The most important, the clitoral nub, is about a half-inch outside and above the vagina. This nub, or button, has far more erotic nerve endings than even the head of your penis.

Without stimulating this, it is unlikely you will bring the woman to the point of orgasm. One has to pay attention in order to stroke the nub because of its position. One has to position oneself in such a way to stroke outside and above the vagina with the shaft of the penis. Make sure you know if you are stimulating acceptably.

The rest of the clitoris erogenous zone, the clitoral wishbone, surrounds the vagina just inside the walls of the opening. This is the other most important erotic zone for the woman.

While it is not a challenge to stroke with the shaft, bringing the head of the penis into contact with the clitoral wishbone is another level of stimulation for the woman. Do not even attempt it until you have mastered the basics discussed above.

Bang! You are now human. You should be able to learn to last as long as *she* desires. You can finally feel successful at the most transcendent act of human life.

I wish I could be around for the next hundred years or so, as all of this flourishes. I just know there are mountains more learning that will occur once men's terrible inhibitions, frustrations, and emasculations are shredded as loving coitus truly and finally becomes celebrated as it always should have been and is transformed into a loving art form.

It is the most important art form of love that will replace the grubbing ways in which sex is treated today.

I've had many women mention how it is all about the missing affection in men that is the problem. That is what drives women crazy and away. What women have never realized is that missing affection stems from the same problem.

How can a man not become inhibited in his expression of affection and love as he fails at the most essential act of making love? How can he maintain an affectionate demeanor when failing to express it in the most meaningful way in bed?

The man may feel utterly disappointed in the situation, as well as himself, feeling like he has already betrayed the woman he desires to show his love. Many a man will close up, once his failure to express his love in the most meaningful physical manner begins to sink in. It sinks in so insidiously many never even become aware of it. It can become a haunting feel that won't go away but, also, won't surface.

Yes, some overcome the shock. Some find other ways. You cannot tell me they are not disappointed all the same.

Men take, women give and it all starts in bed. It doesn't need to remain that way.

I will say, once again, kudos to guys that find some other way to satisfy their partner, kudos to those that have taken a completely different route to find love. I'm sure your affection is far more than those that never learned to love in whatever way is possible and works best for the couple. But, still, until loving coitus is a reality that mankind accepts and proliferates, it is a humbled existence at which any primate could succeed. Only with loving coitus do we separate ourselves decisively from the animals.

I mention exercises. It is in some detail below. There are also plenty of Kegel exercises available on the web. Just keep in mind that there are two parts to the exercise. The second will not be mentioned in any reference to Kegel exercises. The first is to exercise those muscles to make them supple and responsive. The *second* is to *not* exercise those muscles while exercising the muscles that are *meant* for movement in your thighs, torso, etc. in order to become familiar with the separation of efforts. I like my exercises better because they only take a couple of minutes.

Regarding masturbation (I explain more below). Do not abuse your member. That is even worse than any bad habits you can pick up from masturbation. On bad habits, do not let the habit of thinking only about your own causing your own orgasm during masturbation prevent you from thinking about the woman's during the actual event of coitus.

Your main goal *has* to be the woman's orgasm during coitus. You orgasm is assured, hers is not. Habits are hard to break.

I have left as much of my original details below because I am concerned that this is a difficult enough subject as it is. Reiteration in different words may help. I have not edited much.

Original Details

Men have always accepted that starting the process of ejaculation was impossible to avoid. Because of this misconception, it became a matter of attempting to *stop the end result*. ***Big mistake.*** That is far too late. It became something similar to an olympic event in most men's minds. More strength is not the answer. More control is.

The big picture is that the sex glands in the crotch, when squeezed, begin ejaculation. Nothing else. That's it.

Two instincts trigger the sex glands by squeezing them. It has been 'a mystery' before now. So much for mystery.

Men learned only to hold on for dear life *after* the process of ejaculation has already begun. That assures the two or three minute limit that is de rigueur in sex studies. A study of the anatomy and the characteristics of the act of coitus is much more enlightening. There is no limit.

The unfortunate results of uncontrolled ejaculation ends the act of coitus before it can ever become a loving, thereby, human event that creates the loving environment that is necessary to fulfill our humanity. Uncontrolled ejaculation is a disaster. It is prehuman. It is not necessary and highly destructive to relationships and the human race.

By studying the anatomy in the context of erection, ejaculation and some of the oddities of results of masturbation, it becomes clear. Squeezing the sex glands in the pubic area (i.e. the crotch, the pelvic region) begins the process of ejaculate discharge.

There are two instinctual reactions that cause the witless squeezing of the sex glands in the crotch. They is nothing more than the instincts of the animals that came before us. That knowledge has been shunted aside due to the overwhelming feelings of shame that were first encountered by the first fully awakened sentient intellect more than three millennia ago. Those instincts, when the shame is shunted aside and the intellect finally assesses the real situation, are easy to overcome because we are human, thinking creatures.

One of those instincts is as simple to overcome as it is to understand. Men don't twerk until the lady sings. Thrusting the pubic bone (crotch) forward to the furthest extent squeezes the glands decisively (i.e. twerking). The animal's *instinct* is to immediately plunge as deeply as possible. It just feels good.

In the case of twerking (undisciplined full forward thrust), the musculoskeletal structure forces the pubic bone into a position that squeezes the sex glands. It will invariably cause the beginnings of orgasm, and ejaculation in the man's case.

The second instinct is more subtle. The pelvic muscles *are not required for movement.* They have everything to do with squeezing the sex glands and controlling other bodily output functions. The pelvic muscles do not *need* to flex, unless desired, during the movements of sexual activity. When flexed, they squeeze the sex glands.

The other muscles in the thighs, buttocks, back, and torso, etc are the only necessary muscles for movement. The crotch muscles only flex due to the witless instincts of the animal. They don't do anything regarding movement. They are not used for movement, they just witlessly follow along.

It is just a matter of realizing this and avoiding using the pelvic muscles for the movements involved in loving coitus. This is what I term 'jerking'. It just takes practice.

The two endpoints of the stroke are the most likely to cause those muscles to flex inadvertently, which is where the term jerking originated.

It's not so much leaving them lax as *not flexing them*. Flexing and relaxing those muscles acts like a pump on the glands. The 'tickling' effect on the head of the penis cause the same results through spasming. Mastery of these muscles is key.

The muscle response (jerking) or deep plunge (twerking) squeezes the glands containing the fluids that begins the cascade to orgasm. Save the deep plunge for the finale, when *she* is ready. It will *always* cause ejaculation and orgasm on call within a very short period of time. You can learn how long, also, with practice. It can all be controlled.

Holding on for dear life is *exactly* what a man does *not* want to do as it amounts to *flexing the pelvic muscles*!

One additional critical point. If the glands are *already overfull*, squeezing the glands is unavoidable. The solution is obvious.

Only about two inches is required to stroke the woman's every erotic nerve-ending inside and out, while allowing the head of the penis to remain fully inside the vagina. The shaft itself strokes the most sensitive arousal point (i.e. clitoral nub) that is just *outside* and *above* the opening (by ~ one-half inch or less). The other major erogenous zone for a woman is the clitoral wishbone, much less than two inches inside.

Stroking the clitoral wishbone, just inside the vaginal opening, with the flaring portion of the head will also help stimulate the woman. That may be best saved for after you have learned the basics. The woman's twerking should assist her orgasm in the same way as a man. The two should discuss what works best.

Think on this. Now, once you both begin to achieve orgasm, you can leave the lights on and look into each other's loving eyes as you each achieve the transcendent state of orgasm.

Just be careful and go very slow until you understand 1) how deep is safe (it should be far more than two inches as you progress in your learnings) and 2) how to avoid contracting (or, worse, spasming) the muscles in the crotch.

An additional technique, if necessary, is to stop all activity at the first sign that you are becoming overstimulated until the sense of overstimulation is gone. It should not be necessary with exercise and practice but may be useful while still learning.

It is a learning process. We are human. That is what we do. That is what we are *supposed* to do. In the case of coitus, we have avoided the learning process, thus remaining a dumbfounded animal.

These points are straightforward and will become as natural as the instincts and animal responses that they replace within a generation or two of the time that humanity begins to succeed at love in its most essential physical form. Little real learning should be necessary within a generation or two. It will be absorbed from the confidence of one's elders (which is completely missing today) and, maybe, a few minor insights that will be commonly known, like, "don't twerk, don't jerk, and exercise. Become familiar with the muscles in the crotch and *don't flex them*. Make them supple."

The exercises are just as crucial for loving coitus in youth as it is for later in life. There are other benefits as you age, like not wearing diapers. The immediate advantages, even in youth, include making it easier to master the muscles and any untoward spasming of the muscles. It will take some slight effort and discipline, as well as exercise (two minutes!), to avoid flexing and spasming. Avoiding the deep plunge is just a matter of paying attention. Now, you will be able to open your eyes to the one you adore while actually loving her in the best way.

I spend around *two* minutes (only two!) exercising those muscles daily, and, also, practicing *not* flexing them by only exercising the muscles that *are* necessary for movement.

On your back with knees flexed, swing your knees towards each other and away. Flex the pelvic muscles as you swing the knees towards each other. Relax the muscles as you swing the knees apart. Thirty times, approximately thirty seconds. This will make the muscles supple and help you become familiar with muscles. Then, flex another thirty times while swinging the knees in and out. In this case, leave the crotch muscles relaxed while working only the leg, butt, and hip muscles to get the pelvic muscles familiar with avoiding flexing while the the muscles meant for movement are working. This could also be practiced during walking, sitting, or any form of exercise, though I found it best to be able to concentrate. I've also experimented with variations a bit. One that is intriguing is flexing the pelvic muscles on one count, then leaving them relaxed on the next.

Then, I hold them for a count of five, relax, another five count, relax. Six of these total.

I would also suggest alternating between this exercise and doing them with the legs stretched out fully. Just swinging your toes suffice, in this case.

Another good, errr, non-exercise is standing knee bends *without* flexing the pelvic muscles. What is termed 'sexercise' would be a perfect time to practice this. Tai chi or squats work just as well.

In essence, you are trying to do two things. Condition the pelvic muscles *and* become familiar with *not* using them when unnecessary and detrimental to the act of loving coitus.

I really doubt this will be the last written on exercises to make it easier to avoid unwanted orgasms. I have already rewritten this a dozen times as I learned more and more. I expect there is more yet that others will discover once we remove the blinders.

Another caution. Self-stimulation (or dress rehearsals, or masturbation, if you prefer) needs to be done carefully for the man. If you abuse your member, it will come back to haunt you. *Do not inadvertently do so!* It will make it almost impossible to avoid the beginnings of ejaculation. There is no reason to abuse your member, *if you realize what triggers an orgasm.*

It can be difficult to achieve orgasm when, errr, taking the matter in hand, *because* the normal motions of coitus are *not* the norm during self-stimulation. Also, the tickle response is absent.

A person cannot tickle themselves.

Also, the urge to rush through can become a habit that follows through when attempting to last as long as *she* desires. Do not allow that habit to develop. It is really hard to break. If one uses something other than one's hand, it may be possible to engage the tickle response to some extent and begin to overcome it.

Abuse, which can happen in attempts to cause the tickle response, or rush to completion, will make the spasm response *extremely* difficult to overcome. *Do not abuse your member.*

Humanity should learn to approach masturbation unabashedly. It is far better than letting the lack of release get under one's skin. I'm not expecting that to change in a hurry. Once we lose our sense of shame regarding sex, maybe we will have a chance.

Also, don't let your child (either sex, really) be mutilated by circumcision. In the U.S., it is considered a Christian tradition. IT IS NOT A CHRISTIAN TRADITION!!!! The health aspect is also a crock. It is sadistic. It leaves scars.

There is no rational reason for the mutilation of circumcision (either gender), though there are many irrational, insane reasons.

A circumcised person can still achieve controlled ejaculation but it may be more of a challenge (I was circumcised).

More importantly, the biggest thing for me is that I am certain it leaves a psychic shock when they slice it away, no matter the anesthetics or sharpness of the scalpel. There's just no need for it. It is sick and sadistic. It is an animal reveling in causing pain.

I would say that, no matter where you are in the world, it would be worth checking before you have a baby. In many places (the U.S. south), they will slice without asking.

Just remember, you are human. Of course you can control the muscles and your own discharge. Keep in mind that overfull glands means they *will* be squeezed and it will be over in a hurry. How you handle that is up to you.

Do not become discouraged if it takes a little while to adjust and make things work. At this point, it is all new. The older you are, the more time should be expected in order to adjust as there are more bad habits necessary to overcome.

You can now proceed to engage in loving coitus, mutual orgasm, enthusiastically in a human manner while gazing into your lover's eyes with the lights on. Love can finally mature into its sentient form. We can become human. Rather than a porn-watching subhuman race. I apologize for concentrating on the men's issues but men have the most to learn, by far.

There is another point that I have not highlighted before. The closest I came was mentioning that, after men gain their confidence, their self-respect, the rest will come easily.

While that is true, it is not enough, at this point. During the transition into that state, there are a few things that a man will need to consider. After we are human, it will be as obvious as the Earth beneath your feet.

Not only does a woman's orgasm take some time but, at least at this point, so does arousal for many women. I think it is very possible that this, also, will change, once women become convinced that they, also, can expect to achieve orgasm during coitus on a consistent basis. Their enthusiasm may often even match that of the man.

The point is that, if a man does not take his time achieving the woman's high arousal, before beginning coitus, she may never achieve orgasm. I would love to see a book by a woman on these matters. The orientation for a man needs to change radically. It is not all about him. It is all about loving and giving, not just pleasing oneself.

For women, just make sure you are doing the opposite of what I've recommended for men and you should orgasm easily. Flex and twerk like crazy or as much as he can bear, which should improve over time. Relish the erotic feelings that cause the spasms to engage. Again, I would dearly love to see a woman write a book on the woman's sexual situation and insights.

I am becoming more and more convinced that, as we open up and become more comfortable with the change and the insights, we will learn a lot more.

All of this will become natural once we remove the blinders. We will no longer be in hiding, and we can look for further ways in which to improve the loving. I don't mean just the physical aspects, either. This book will become unnecessary soon.

As an example of the other aspects to explore further, I'll mention romance and, of course, foreplay. Those are other natural aspects of being human that have been inhibited by men's inability to love physically, his shame.

Once our natural desire to love is established and reinforced by men gaining confidence that they can love, the rest of our loving nature will flourish. This goes well beyond the intimate relationship, as well. Humanity can become a balanced, emotionally stable, rational loving race of sentient beings without the over-heightened paranoia and despair.

A few further notes as I progress even further. First of all, after six books I am annoyed to find that the excellent term that I had created, indefinitely delayed ejaculation, 1) is not unique, and 2) has been already adopted to cover the case of the poor man that can't ever ejaculate or, goodness forbid (yeah, still despise using the term 'god' in any form), might last long enough to pleasure his woman with orgasm.

Secondly, there is a lot better term: controlled ejaculation.

I haven't even touched on any of the subjects besides men lasting long enough that are crucial to making love. The rest of it will come easily, once men are certain that they don't need to fail at the most essential task: lasting long enough. In the meantime, though, as we seek our way, it is at least worth mentioning a few key points.

The rest is easy, if you consider it at all, but still worth noting. The emotional loving, the affectionate responses and attitudes; the romance, the foreplay, the loving attitude, the gentle, equitable treatment of women, the rainbow loving of women that has been lacking, all falls right out of what I have been explaining. Men must just put their shame behind them.

Also, remember, it is the woman that gets pregnant, not you. So, if coitus is off the table, deal with it. If you care for her enough, you'll stick around. Find some other way in which to achieve mutual orgasm.

I have to highlight, though, that there are other ways to *assure* (a condom is not assurance; the woman being forced to futz with her hormones by taking a pill is not, either, besides, futzing with her physiology and mental state) impregnation never takes place while engaging in coitus.

Admissions and extensions

Everything above in this chapter has been proved to my own satisfaction. It was more difficult than most any man should encounter from this point forward. That is the point in explaining all of this. The effort is not difficult. Just overcoming the brainwashing and avoidance of the issue was difficult.

In a number of ways, it was more difficult for me. I had no template. I was encumbered by all of the lies, misdirections, and utter suppression of the subject that have burdened mankind for millennia. I was also circumcised. I also had damage to the head of my penis prepubescence and, worst of all, I had abused my member.

I have now provided a basic template to move forward and avoid all of the pitfalls that I encountered over a lifetime *before* I realized it was all a sham almost too late to prove the case to myself.

I realize this does not prove the case for all men. That will take some time and effort by others to show that it is not an isolated case and expand on the basic template that I have provided. The point of the previous two paragraphs is to emphasize that I am no one special when it comes to making loving coitus.

Everything I have to add, from this point forward, regarding improving men's performance to the point that they are in full control of the body when it comes to controlling, errr, coming, and mastering their bodies has no proof, other than I have spent the last dozen years pondering it all and linking many, many obscure dots.

These insights came far too late for me to prove them out with any level of certainty. I have no proof they help but they are rational considerations, in some cases, extrapolations from previous insights *that did work*. Some, points below, are just clarifications.

I am way to friggin' old now to be able to 'test them out' with any validity. But, they make sense.

I have to start by stressing that we are only just beginning, so there will be a lot more to learn as we progress and shed the blinders.

Humanity never stops improving on anything that it (finally) takes seriously. Loving coitus will become far more than the clinical analysis that I have had to provide. It will become art. It will expand the art of loving into something more human, once the unnecessary fear and shame are put away.

None of this will be necessary at all as men begin to gain confidence in their ability to love.

It's just that hangover of deluding ourselves for three millennia that continues to concern me. So, the more thorough the explanation and understanding, the easier it will be for all men to get over the hurdle of the debacle of our past that has prevented the human race from loving fully.

On the topic of exercise, I want to stress *not* to follow any rule book. You may start with my suggestions but find what works best for you. I would be shocked in the extreme if people don't find even better ways to strengthen and train those muscles.

I lost along the way through the many books one interesting technique that can be used while learning to master one's body. Moving the whole body, rather than flexing the hips in any way, or not moving any portion of the *man's* body are two ways to avoid squeezing those glands. I'll leave it at that for your exploration. Then, the one element of spasming in response to the erotic sensation can be concentrated on.

Sometimes I think of it like this door that men have always considered locked against them. Now, as we push gently against it, we find it is wide open. Quit letting the fears of your ancient ancestors prevent you from realizing you are a human. You can love a woman the way you have always desired.

One of the most crucial points that I cannot emphasize enough is that it is about a man changing his focus and, thereby, his behaviour from that of an animal to that of a human. That is the real point of all of this. Men's humanity has been hampered.

The laser focus for every man needs to become that it is about *sharing* the love in its physical form. All of the myriad forms of love can flourish from that point forward.

This is where the discussion becomes more speculative. As I mentioned with twerking, it is the whole musculoskeletal structure that kicks in to squeeze those glands in your crotch. I think there may be another way in which the musculoskeletal structure can be persuaded to avoid putting pressure on those glands.

Men often have a tendency to point their feet at an angle with the toes away from each other. I think there is a distinct possibility that one's toes being closer together than one's heels might very well cause the musculoskeletal structure to become less prone to squeezing the sex glands. It seems like it makes more room for the glands.

More so, as I studied it further, it strengthens the muscles on the inside of the thigh if one walks with the toes pointed slightly inward.

I have another exercise that I do. It is bending at the hips with the legs and back straight. When doing the exercise with the toes closer together than the heels, I can feel those back, inner thigh muscles stretching. I am beginning to believe that these muscles also need to be strengthened in order to make it easier to avoid using the crotch muscles during coitus. Just a theory.

I would appreciate a word if things begin to start working better for you. As I have said, I am the only verified person to succeed at this, so far.

Men

It's hard to believe I have more to say but, blame it on three millennia of confusion and misdirection. There's a lot of confusion that has mounted over three millennia. All because men were ashamed of something for which they had no reason to be ashamed. They just didn't realize it.

It's sad, really. Men have been embarrassing themselves since the beginning. All that 'master of the universe' stuff that is so popular is the saddest joke that we have played on ourselves.

It is such a sad coverup and for no good reason. Just accepting that the woman deserves the same sexual fulfillment as the man would be a huge step. But, I'm not big on small steps. Therefore, Details.

I cannot get over the stark confusion that we have endured for thousands of years. *That* is embarrassing for the whole species of human.

I could never comprehend the desperate grasping that humanity pursued with not the slightest sense. Now, I've got it. It is all because we have zero confidence in ourselves. That's gotta end. We are sentient and there is only one thing holding us back.

It's amazing to me! After fifty years, I finally see childhood and puberty clearly.

How can it be that a sentient race assure itself that the children go into their sexual lives completely unprepared. In some countries, all of the horrors and none of the incredible feelings, emotionally volley, and that most incredible experience of a lifetime are swept under the rug, never to be mentioned.

That has to seems strange to you, *I hope!*

After three millennia, one would think we would have learned something. All we've learned is to lie to ourselves about the sexual situation. So, we fumble on, embarrassing ourselves further.

Maybe this is a good place to start. Sex is *not (YET!)* all it has been promoted to be. It is usually a nasty little affair with both skulking to some extent. So, of course, no one wants to talk about it.

It always cracks. Sooner or later, the dishonesty regarding the sexual situation comes home to roost on the relationship. No one even notices the core to all of the dismay.

The cracks are showing. They are showing at a level never before allowable. It's all breaking. All because we wouldn't admit that we had something to learn about loving.

The physical love may be a casual relationship but, at its heart, it is so much more. More than any other aspect of life, it affects the heart *and the head* with a wallop as long as we keep avoiding the current conclusion: men are a bust at loving. Once we accept that, we can move on.

We can, then, realize that it's all been a cockup because we never even looked.

Transition

There will be some thoughts in this section that may seem over the top. They will remain.

That's it for covering what was written in the previous ten books. Believe me, there is a lot more in the other books. The topic that I was dying to put in here is misogyny. To me, misogyny is the worst, most blatant evidence that something is wrong. It also points the way to what is wrong.

What continues to amaze me is that no one wants to admit that misogyny is the male gender's problem. Not individuals but the whole gender, even if some few make nice.

I could have just suggested that mutual pleasure was the answer, which is true. But, it is not enough. Coitus must become a respectable engagement. For me, that always meant loving coitus. The option of accepting it as only a way in which to make babies, and that we really need other avenues for love, left a bad taste in my mouth. Also, it leaves men wondering why they can't do better. We are sentient. Of course we can do better!

I am incredibly happy that I got to the bottom of it all. To realize that our sentience lays as much in making coitus a loving act as it is men overcoming the complex reason that it fails - ***in a sentient manner***. That is crucial.

There is something about overcoming the instincts of an animal that unleashes more than I ever imagined.

I believe, now, that it is the lever that launches us into a whole new dimension of life. Love is almost a side-benefit.

We have been in a stupour for three millennia. All because we could not face the facts when it comes to sex. Besides all of the frustration of the last few millennia, the stupour stunted so much.

We would peer out with little insights regarding our existence, but the stupour always kept us from thinking anything through. That has made a train wreck of our existence. Can't you see it in all of the snake-oil salesman's tactics with which this life remains littered? Once you look closely, you will see it everywhere.

So, maybe what I am saying is the unleashing of our intellect in tandem with a stable human perspective, that includes love, is going to be something to see. I think it would even surprise me and I am ready for a lot.

As men get over the chip on their shoulder because they are no longer lousy at sex, it frees up *everything*. As men no longer feel threatened by the sexual situation, men, women, and their relationships will transform into something remarkable. The human race will transform into something remarkable.

It is all about humanity gaining its self-respect and self-confidence.

I never really thought about the fact that both genders have been stunted. When the finer qualities of both genders are on display I cannot even describe what I expect. It is something to be lived, not just ruminated.

I am not wrong. All on down the line, I am right. That makes it worth a little more effort on my part.

Big picture

Sometimes I wonder if I am the only one that can even consider the big picture. Everyone seems to get so caught up in the minutiae that the big picture is not even in view. We talk sustainability, *acts* of misogyny, but no one is willing to face the fact that humanity itself is completely off target.

It is shocking to me that humanity keeps trying to blame misogyny on the few individuals that get caught. I explain our flawed perspective on misogyny throughout my books. So, don't consider the following a through explanation. I just feel it might help.

There is one example that I think defines the misogyny situation well. That movie director that saw roasted for it. I'm not excusing him but I wonder how many can really conceive of the situation?

A man is put in a powerful position. Some women are willing to go to exceptional lengths to get a powerful man's attention. Let's take the least offensive male. One that is not tied down to any woman. How many men do you really think would not be tempted to get carried away? Even if they had a significant other? Few would decline those women that throw themselves at powerful men. That is the very sick and attractive feature of becoming a powerful man. Attract women even though you are lousy at sex. It is a gender wide phenomenon whether it is indulged by all or not. That is closer to the big picture. Something is wrong when both men and women betray their self-respect for petty reasons.

Think about the most numerous ads on almost any site nowadays. Unless the site itself can balance the desire for more money with some shred of self-respect. They always use men's titillation to sell. It is nothing other than pornography in a slightly more subtle form. Revealing décolletage, hints at sexy pictures. It's truly sick and we indulge it more and more as our sentient awareness gets beaten further into submission to the animal.

It is using the trepidation of the animal when it comes to sex to sell, SeLL, SELL. Because it's always been that way, we believe there is no recourse.

It's not that our self-respect shouldn't be tested. It is that our self-respect should not crumble at the drop of a hat.

Shaman

If I feel like any mystical figure, I like to think Shaman. I am not a prophet, in that I don't predict the future. I do try to get a vague image of what it will mean to be truly human but no more.

To me, it's kind of a silly prospect. It is much more important to understand what is going on than what it might lead to.

My time has been spent more like a Shaman at an intense level of thought for most of my lifetime. I have been observing, cataloging, and linking events for a very long time. I mention directly above that I think the stupour has been a problem. What I mean by that is that we are all capable of an intense level of thought.

I was able to maintain a ridiculous level of intense thought. Not something that I hope anyone has to repeat. I was able to do that because I was content with my humanity. Part of my ability to be one smart dude is that nothing bothered me enough to intrude on my contended state. Only the failure to love a woman and the awful behaviour of humans intruded on my contentedness. It finally intruded in a big way.

What I'm trying to explain is that I didn't let anything get in the way of sentient thought to a degree that disabled sentient thought. I never fell for the stupour; the deceits, distractions, and the delusions. Even the resultant confusion hardly touched me until it bowled me over.

As long as I was convinced it was a small number of men that were lousy at coitus, that happened to include me, I could remain content. Just the breaks, so to speak. I just had to cope with it. It's really more complicated than that but, I guess, I just looked at it all as one vast puzzle. Life was good but something was wrong. The curious behaviour of men was a riddle.

When it hit me that the *vast majority* of men are lousy at unassisted coitus, it all just fell in place. 1) We were screwed up. 2) Men are lousy at coitus. 3) ***AND***, no one was willing to admit openly that there was something wrong with the sexual landscape. Do you get it? We surrendered to the animal because we could not make sex into something human.

We couldn't face the reality of a sentient being, so we bent and twisted it out of all proportion and perspective of a human sentient, potentially loving and emotionally stable race.

The growing awareness of the gender-wide inability also led to the stunning realization that it has all been a farce. A thinking human is not an animal so there is no reason to expect it to act like one and, yet, that is the farcical existence we have tolerated since the beginning.

Below is nothing but some crazy thoughts that I have not been able to pursue in depth because I've been a bit busy saving your asses. I just wish to let it out.

I started this all in such a selfless way. I picked the big problem of humanity rather than the small problem of my own inadequacy. As I state elsewhere, I guess I accepted that it was just my problem. It was also so hidden by all of the pokes and prods applied to all of us in our youth that suggest you just don't think about it. Or, maybe a better description is a naive way.

The more I look at it, the more dizzying it gets. Because the instincts of an animal were too much for our ancient ancestors to handle, we have spent the last three millennia in thrall to the animal.

I finally uncovered a selfish reason that I don't mind so much. If I succeed in making humanity see what is going on, whickwithy will be remembered forever.

Funny thing. I would rather that whickwithy was remembered than me. I want it to stay anonymous. It could have been anyone of us. In some ways, I think of whickwithy as humanity or Gaia maybe. You should read my poem on the subject.

The reality is becoming more striking every day. I have always been fascinated that no one could conceive of humanity becoming something more than a grubbing animal, in any literature I have read (read that as any written or spoken word that I have encountered). Even scifi uses characters just as damaged as humans are today. No one even seems to contemplate the idea that we can be something far different than we are today.

The reality of what we can become is becoming clearer every day. It is awesome. So, does it surprise you that I have this tremendous ache because it seems impossible for me to be able to convey to humanity that it can overcome that hump - in this lifetime? The dumbfounded features of our current existence are even beyond my estimations.

I don't want to get into all of the technical reasons it is becoming increasingly clear that I will not get it done in this lifetime. The point is that I have had two driving factors for the last many years. The first is that humanity can attain its humanity and I can help it along to realization. The second is that I had not yet completely understood the problem to its last grain of dust.

Both are failing to hold true any longer. Maybe I've nudged things along ... or not. I certainly don't feel I have the heart to continue.

It's magic

We live in a physical realm. While a couple can effuse their love for one another all day long, when it doesn't happen between the sheets, it all falls apart. As long as the most natural way in which it can happen doesn't exist, as long as men think that it is difficult to consummate the act of loving coitus, we are lost.

The ease with which a man can overcome the instincts of an animal is all explained on the blogspot available on my profile in the post Details.

It becomes infinitely easier once we quit hiding from the issue.

Men seek to extend the loving event a few minutes while the truth is that they can extend it as long as *she* desires or exhaustion takes him. The act of a man's own orgasm is completely under a man's own control. He just doesn't know it yet.

Do you want to know why men obsess so much about control? It is because they have not been able to control the one loving event for which they so desperately desire to control. The loving event of coitus. They will remain lost until they face that fact.

- There is no simple way to convey the problem (singular) that humanity faces.

Men are undermined when they fail at the physical act of love. They are diminished. When men fail at loving a woman physically in some manner, they fail utterly at being human.

Women are also aware of the failure, of course. They do not make a big deal out of it because it's not their place to do so, but that doesn't make things any better. No matter how understanding a woman is, her lack of success at achieving the transcendental state during coitus begins to wear. Most women want to love a man just as much as most men want to love a woman but it cannot be sustained over a lifetime when the physical act of love is diminished. All aspects of love become an act. Love loses its meaning. Men are most diminished because their emotional love becomes compromised as the inability to make it real in the physical realm abides.

It becomes infinitely easier once we quit hiding from the issue. It also becomes infinitely easier once a man realizes that there are no time limits.

- In one of my books I suggested that the *failure to achieve loving coitus* was like a pebble that caused an avalanche leading to our bestial behaviour.

It may be more accurate to say that, *until the failure of loving coitus is overcome*, we will remain in the dregs of the bestial past from which we evolved.

Maybe best is to say that *loving* coitus releases our humanity.

We are no longer an animal in toto. That makes for an utter mess as long as we retain the idea that coitus is, almost invariably, a sentient loving failure still ruled by an animal's perspective that a few minutes is the best a man can expect.

Coitus' success as a sentient act of love creates the conditions for another level of existence far beyond the animal once the pebble is released - or the tipping point is reached, as Malcolm Gladwell would say. That is to say that the act of coitus becomes a sentient loving event for enough men to start the avalanche. Once men realize they can love, we become human.

The ease with which a man can overcome the instincts of an animal is explained in the post 'Detail' on the blogspot available at my profile.

It becomes infinitely easier once we quit hiding from the issue. It also becomes infinitely easier once a man realizes that there are no time limits, only exhaustion. Pursuing two minutes was always fool's gold. It becomes possible once we realize that it is only a matter of overcoming an animal's instincts which a human male can easily do. We think.

There's a lot to unpack. If you are a man, start with 'Details'. It's just a matter of overcoming an animal's instincts which is only a matter of physiology.

\- That which must happen for humanity to attain its humanity is for enough men to prove to themselves that loving coitus is simple and human. The rest will follow.

We think. We are human. There is no reason in the world that the instincts of an animal cannot be overcome with ease. They just have to be understood first. You are welcome.

\- Men seek to extend the loving event a couple of minutes while the truth is that they can extend it as long as *she* desires or exhaustion takes him. It is all completely under a man's own control. He just doesn't know it yet.

Do you want to know why men obsess so much about control? It is because they have not been able to control the one loving event for which they so desperately desire control. The loving event of coitus. They will remain lost until they face that fact. It is foolishness to think a human cannot succeed.

\- In all of this, I am not saying it will be easy for the first few men to overcome their certainty that they can never do better than a few minutes.

It is not so difficult to learn. It is difficult to undo the inaccurate learnings of the many millennia in which we were convinced we could do no better than an animal at coitus.

\- Don't ever believe that things will change because a few men achieve loving coitus. Things won't begin to change until the gender of modern man realizes that loving coitus is the only human version. Everyone of them.

Even that is only the beginnings of digging ourselves out of the hole we have continued to dig for millennia. The next step seems most likely the flourishing of the loving treatment of women followed by women coming out of the bunker they have inhabited for millennia.

- I fear that a lot of people cannot comprehend the importance of the idea that a gender can change its mind.

In everything I have written, that is the underlying assumption. It is not a matter of a few men learning how to love. The gender's understanding must be that it knows how to love in a physical manner.

It is similar to walking or talking. These are expected of any human, unless fate intervenes. The same must become true of love in its physical form, loving coitus.

- What I finally realized about myself is that, whatever it is, I have to get it off my chest. Especially lies. There is one lie that precedes all the rest. Men have no option but to be lousy at coitus and loving. That is a flat-out lie.

- The reason that men are so prone to the vulnerability of guilt finally hit me. They have always known they were guilty of scuttling the loving event of coitus. Due to their feelings of helplessness regarding the situation, they can easily take on guilt by the boatload. That leads to a poor image of the male.

- If you are a woman and you are with a man you like a lot, I would take a long time to consider if good coitus would improve your state. The reason for the deep consideration is whether you should broach the subject with your significant other. I know a lot of women that I would not recommend broaching the subject. I'm not sure I know any that should.

I am certain of the prospects for loving coitus but it is a big step for someone to take to attempt the effort. It will take a man with a resolute mind that is willing to face failure in order to attempt to love.

One needs to consider whether one should discuss what I suggest in 'Details'. It all has to do with the mechanics, the plumbing if you will, of the man's act of coitus. From a theoretical standpoint, it makes sense. I proved it to myself *before* I learned the mechanics, so I know it will work.

It takes a very sturdy mind to accept the burden of admitting that one has something to learn about an act that seems so natural (which, by the way, is why we haven't broached the subject in three millennia of coherent sentient existence; and, also why we went so screwy about sex).

The short span of coitus is natural for an animal. But, you wouldn't ask an animal (or me) to play baseball. You wouldn't ask one to drive a car or do mathematics. It is natural for a human to supersede an animal.

As a woman, take a look at 'Details', if your relationship is stable enough. It's like riding a bike for a man. We just never comprehended the instincts and physiological facts that drive it all.

-

I have to add that I expect improvements in the explanations that I have provided in Details. I also expect an even deeper understanding as we progress.

- This is residing close to my heart right now.

What will I want to read as a sentient being?

Since I straddle the two realms in this late stage of my life, as I discern between that which has been instilled into me for seventy years by our prehuman condition and the freedom from the nonsense that I acquired on my own, the question becomes more ponderous.

As I put away the issues and conceptions of our insane behaviour and envision a sane humanity, I find it difficult to engage in any of the usual suspects for reading. History, technical, scientific, astronomic, fiction, even sci-fi begins to pale. There is only one way I ever find the answer. It wont't come in the fading years of this life.

While I'm not sure what I will desire to read, my guess is that music will make a big play in any future life.

I can't, for the life of me, think of any sentient reading material other than that which educates in a formal manner that will remain interesting. It's tricky. I guess it's most likely that the reading material of a fully sentient race will be radically different. My guess is that it will be complemented by a huge difference in how we educate, as well.

- Gods were created when the misery became unbearable. They will vanish alongside the landscape of misery.
- I mentioned before that I have asked myself a question often over the last decade, as I isolated further and further from all humanity. Do I despise humanity? The answer always comes back a resounding, "*No!*" The question has continued to bother me, though. I can now accurately explain with some precision. I think one perspective of mine was critical for me to get this far. I never hated myself. I loved myself thoroughly. I hated the circumstances. Being blindsided by the utterly failed act of coitus is debilitating. Yes, yes, yes, if you are a comfortably blind idiot animal, you can convince yourself that everything is alright with coitus. It makes babies, just like any dull-witted animal should expect.

It blunted my life. It blunted my sentience. The same goes for the bulk (all but one) of humanity. I don't hate anyone. I love them all with all my heart. I just can't cope with everyone's delusions any more than I could tolerate them in my own case.

That forced me into isolation to figure out what had gone wrong. It wasn't me. It isn't even the rest of the people that I have encountered. It is only the circumstances that follow us around like an awful shadow. One woman brought out that sympathy for circumstances and the pain it causes more than anyone else. She knows who she is.

- I remain in fascinated regarding one aspect of this journey. I had a lot of physical damage done to my body. In some ways, it feels like it represents all of the pain that humanity endures. The reason I say that is that, as I broke through all of the nonsense that we endure, I have also, seemingly simultaneously, slowly broken through the physical pain. It's kinda weird. All of the damage had to do with the bones. It hit its peak when a big toe I smashed in my youth froze up to the point it was difficult to walk about a dozen years ago.

That was at about the same time I figured out all of the nonsense. It probably preceded the breakthrough regarding the nonsense by a couple of years. I was walking twelve miles a day for nearly a decade in order to break that toe free. I had been working on my skeletal structure (back, hips, shoulders, knees, etc) since my teens. To give you a little perspective, in my teens, if I sneezed, I collapsed on the floor because of the resultant damage to the body. My body is now near factory perfection. All that is left is a knob on the outside of my big toe's knuckle causing some little discomfort.

It makes sense, really. I was just healing my own body and mind. It's just that the same mental pain that I encountered was matched by everyone I met. Maybe I just felt that pain to a far greater degree as it was amplified by it reflection in the physical pain and my own deep abiding honesty.

But, that brings up the concept of empathy. I feel like empathy is what attempted to crush me. Was it all just my own pain combined with an unusual sensitivity? What is that sensitivity? Is it just heightened awareness? Awareness of cues that are so subtle most miss them? I have to think that is the case.

In actuality, I don't think that sensitivity is at all uncommon. I think it is available to all. I think most learn quickly and well enough to turn it off in their youth. All of the contention of prehuman life is enough to make most anyone turn it off, if possible.

Another good reason to move on to our humanity.

- I was just thinking about incel and the like. "Involuntarily Celibate" kinda says it all. They know how bad they are at coitus and they hate it. They'll never admit it, but that's the case. So, they have difficulty pursuing a woman, just as I did. I just never blamed it on the woman. All I ever concluded until about a dozen years ago was that something was wrong and it makes life an upheaval. I took care of it myself and never learned to hate. I just learned that the whole race is confounded, dumbstruck.

All of our beliefs regarding sex are in question. All of them.

In answer to incel, get over it and learn to love. The ongoing atrophy of our humanity and its source is reflected in incel. It shows the helplessness that all men feel, though none would ever admit it. And, there is the heart of the problem. Over the millennia, it wore us down.

Incel also reflects the maddening need for male-female relationships that really work rather than scraping along on the border of sanity all the while, wearing away our sanity further by the second.

The most interesting question regarding both sex and human life is freedom. The real, essential freedom we desire is to be freed of the animal. That answers all questions on the subject of freedom.

The myriad misconceptions regarding sex stagger me more every moment. I was just thinking of the old saw, "Men and women are like oil and water." "I've had roommates for X number of year without a problem." or "Men are from Mars and Women are from Venus". Now, do you see the truth?

Even if I were wrong about men's capability, which I assure you I am not, it is better to have it out in the open. If the only purpose of coitus is to make babies, then we would have to face that fact and deal with it. What we have been doing is finding alternatives without admitting the fact that *one* reason we do so is because coitus doesn't cut it. Yes, there may be others.

Just to make sure you don't get confused. Many women have learned to despise men, in general. What they actually despise is the lack of love that is typical of the male. Because of that lack of love, the male acts toxic.

Do you see what I'm saying? When males are no longer toxic because they can love in a physical manner, the women will have no reason to despise them.

This brings up another fascinating disparity between the two genders. Women can't even imagine what it is like to fail to love their significant other in a physical manner. They cannot imagine how awful it feels nor the resultant frustration, anxiety, and angst. Women just see the results: toxic masculinity. I know I am still not being totally clear on this and it's important. I can only hope that some women get what I am saying.

- I am very glad I am not wrong. No matter what, the situation would remain messy without coital resolution. I would guess it would remain a complete mess.

For those loud and well-programmed advocates of LGBTQetc, I'll reiterate one of my favorite insights. Heterosexuals that are engaging in *loving* coitus will not care in the slightest what anyone else is doing to fulfill themselves.

Okay, this is new. We will be able to have open conversations regarding sex, and especially coitus, for the first time in history - without all of the angst and hurt feelings, once we accept reality. There will also be a lot of head shaking. What is currently spewed across the headlines is not a conversation. It's taking some ludicrous side in some nonsensical argument.

As we become more human, we will be having a lot less of all of the taking sides on any subject. I can see governments and organizations (most often led by idiots) that rein in the current insanity transformed into organizations that represent powerful tools to provide for humanity's improvement.

This will, of course, require an entirely sane race. That's the point, really.

- This may be weirdest of all but I am sensing a change in my relationship with Nature. All I can say is that I don't think we will be fighting Mother Nature much longer. Respect will be the order of the day. For Mother Nature, for a sentient race, for yourself and humanity as a whole.

Where do we go from here

One of the places that a sentient race will be able to explore with much improved clarity is our desires.

Everything will get so much better because we will no longer need to lie about our desires. The going thought is that men only desire their own fulfillment. Don't be naive. They *learn* to fulfill *only* their own desires because they fail to provide the fulfillment to their mate. That leads to their selfish perspective. They do not fulfill their mate (during coitus) because they are convinced it is not possible. Not because they are idiots that have no potential for love. It just atrophies from the point of puberty.

Think about it this way. Coitus is required for procreation. For an animal, it was never meant to be a fulfilling prospect. That's why the western churches concluded that sex is just for making babies. They also concluded that our sentience was cursed because we could not make sex into something human, though they never went so far as to state it so brazenly. Sex was such an awful prospect that western churches concluded that their priests should not indulge. Sex was cursed, so how could the (fictional) god's representatives here on Earth partake? No doubt about it. There's a plan that has proved insane.

All of the ways in which we tried to get around the problem (e.g. foreplay, dildo, cunnilingus, LGBTQ, etc) were fine, sort of a compromise with our sentience. If you look at our history, it is clear. None of it cleared the decks of our problems. If you can't see, yet, that loving coitus sweeps the decks clean, I have failed.

We became confused between what we wanted and what we needed. Sheesh! I've mentioned before how all of this is reflected in the songs we sing. My favorite example of this particular one is probably London Grammar's song on the subject. Hanna was dead right in her summation of wants and needs ... and it breaks us as long as the two remain isolated.

We need sexual release. For men, it is crazy important. For women, I couldn't say, but it is beneficial. They have learned to mask their feelings so well that I'm not even sure how many know what they really want or need. Men clearly haven't a clue as to what they really want. They just bury the disappointment so deep in order to *attempt* to remain sane. It doesn't work. It still grates.

One thing is abundantly clear: we want love. Every single one of us wants love. Men learn to live without it and women just seem mystified by it all (and rightly so).

When it is denied (which is essentially *always* in our current conditions), love cannot flourish. That is why older folks most often haven't much love left in their systems. It wears away at each one of us over a lifetime.

This is a fine point that I have tried to stress because it can mislead a lot of people if they have not studied these subjects thoroughly as I have.

Love does not wither on the vine when it is not consummated but it is destroyed when it fails. In other words, in a world in which a man engaging with a woman is certain to succeed at making it a loving event, those that do not find someone with whom to engage do not go crazy. They are supported by a human-wide culture of love.

If some follow the beat of a different drummer, who cares? Not any heterosexual that is fully satisfied with the state of their own sexual lives.

Don't get confused because I use the word love, either. It is not a depiction of some la-la land, some utopia. It is just the depiction of a sane human race based in the advanced form of caring that is essential for a sentient race. It includes loving coitus.

It's not like I am closing doors. I am only opening the one that provides balance and sanity.

Most importantly, we need unfettered love to blossom into our sentient awareness.

Men will not be whole until they realize they can love a woman as our sentience knows damn well they can. Once that becomes the reality, love will flourish.

Tangents

I think I've said all there is to say on how we become human. I can't imagine I could explain it better.

Sigh. But, I've thought that before. In the meantime...

I decided to move on to the frontier of our sentience and see what I can deduce about it. This is all, at this time, open to interpretation and re-thinks. I am no prophet. Just looking for clues.

Just like it took me ten books to explain three millennia (or one billion years, depending on how you desire to count), these are not finished thoughts. I'm not even sure there should be such a term as a finished thought. I am more and more convinced that, whatever realization of reality we achieve, there is more ahead. We just need to quit lying to ourselves.

This is just the best I can do with the tools available and the perspicacity that I have developed at this point in time.

Wow! It's been a lonely existence! I mean lonely! I always said it was an alone existence and I was okay with that. I guess I knew that going in. But, the dizzying array of what could have been if love were fulfilled makes me now feel lonely.

I was attracted by the peacefulness of isolation in our current state of insanity. That's been growing since I was twenty and sitting in that bus station in Bangor on my way to Boston. Being free of the stupid expectations of those around me was liberating.

And, again, Wow! I was just thinking of all of the landmines that I have had to sidestep. It is the reason it has taken me eleven books as I realize I still may not have written it well enough for the dull-witted animal to accept.

I had to attempt to avoid setting off so many triggers that the animal put in place when explaining that we have not attained a sentient sate. The landmines were set long, long ago. If you want to know how far back a landmine of misinterpretation of our existence goes back in time, just ask the question, how many accept the false premise that it portrays? Is it only within a culture, a continent, the whole human race?

An example of a landmine that is not accepted by all of humanity is the Garden of Eden and all that crock. It suggests that humanity is not natural. It suggests that evil invaded in the form of sentient awareness. That knowing that women should also achieve orgasm is evil. That sex is a curse. You have no idea how offensive I consider that myth.

I assure you, humanity is quite natural. The problem is that there are some qualities of the animal that we have yet to shed. They are *unnatural* for a sentient being. They make a caricature out of human life. We have to abandon the belief that there is anything unnatural about a human being in order to achieve a sentient state, which is the *natural* state for a sentient being.

There are beliefs that go further back and encompass the whole of humanity. Like making coitus into a loving act is too much for men to accomplish. All of humanity's consciousness believes that, even if a few individuals have overcome the obstacle.

- The fact that I finally discovered what is missing from our sentient state, along with the fact that I can't seem to get it across to anyone is quite despairing. What remains to be seen is whether it is only the former that will result.

It is amazing to me that we have accepted this unnatural state for so long. It always amazes me. The problem itself is so clear.

A loving relationship is a great idea. As long as the game was played by an animal, it was just fine without. The animal was caught in the trap of its inability to think and express that thought in words. As long as that was true, the awfulness of rutting was fine. Animals had to procreate and they didn't know any better.

We know better. Look at it without all of the camouflage. Men and women can get along fine - until it comes to sex. The excuses we use for the bitterness between men and woman do not hold up. They do not stand on their own.

The man wants sex often for most of their lifetime. Since it is not such a transcendent experience for the woman, they do not. Now, contemplate the results of that most experienced scenario.

That is where it all breaks apart. A thinking woman will not be satisfied with the lack of success of the male to bring her that transcendent experience. They won't be able to tolerate it for a lifetime as often as the man desires. A thinking man knows this and does something about it.

- How do I concisely explain that the ability of a sentient male to love a woman is <u>natural</u> - *for a sentient male?* Once again, I hit a stumbling block.

Do I need to put in "love a woman 'physically'"? I don't see the need but I know everyone will be off in the weeds if I do not. We are not animals. It is *natural* for a sentient being to overcome that which confounds the animal and unleash loving coitus.

Then, I have to deal with all of the landmines *that* sets off with the LGBTQ folks. They will be all out of joint about the connotations that have been heaped on the words 'natural sex'.

Do you even see what I am getting at? Once, you can read that first sentence in this section without being all bent out of shape, no matter who you are, we will be on our way to a sentient state. Once everyone of every persuasion can see what is really being said, and what is really going on, we will be on the doorstep of our sentient state. LGBTQ and everyone else will be off enjoying themselves without any detractors. All of the angst that we all hide away will be gone.

<u>Tickling my brain</u>

There is just so much going on in my head right now that I feel I might explode. It's like, as the barriers come down, the flood of information regarding the truth of our situation is just feeling massively overwhelming.

For instance, this one really shakes me. It is just so out there but there have been too many hints over a lifetime to ignore it. I've always looked at knowledge with suspicion. It is reinforced by so many experiences over a lifetime that got catalogued under "something weird going on here when it comes to knowledge".

One is a game of foosball in which my friend and I were essentially free of thinking things through. In my recollections, which may or may not be very valid, the ball never hit the back walls. It either hit the 'players' feet or the gaol

I'd ask that friend to verify but he's been dead for decades. I ran with a rough crowd for quite a while.

Another was another friend from the same era that went to university because the GI bill was paying the way. He never attended classes and *always* got straight A's. He was shot in the head some few years later.

Another one of those thoughts is the way I have always fought. I was involved in a lot of fights in my youth. It was weird. I was always blindsided by someone wanting to fight me. I was never taught to fight. I didn't know a thing about it and, yet, any fight I have been in (none of which I had anything to do with starting), lasted a few seconds and ended up with the other guy on the ground. One example is this guy who used to be a bully ... until he met me. That first time, I had just moved into the area at about eight years old. I was swinging on a swing in the public area in the middle of the cul de sac. He walked up and told me it was his swing. I don't remember the details, but he attacked. All I remember is me standing over him with one hand on his wrist and the other bending his elbow in the wrong direction. His face was in the ground. How did I know to do that? Altogether, it was a saga of a few weeks. It ended when he invited me to his boxing ring. I knew nothing about boxing, either. I guess he thought that gave him an advantage. He ended up on the ground again with me standing over him mystified.

There are more examples littered throughout my life. There seems to be two solutions. One is reincarnation granting some access to knowledge from previous lives. The other is even weirder. It is that the knowledge is accessible without the drudgery that humanity forces on the situation.

I lean towards the former because the latter is pretty mind-blowing.

- And, here is another fury of mine. It might be what drove more more than anything. Humanity has so much incredible potential, which may be best revealed in the art of music, that it drives me crazy. Everybody should be learning multiple languages, music, poetry as just a side job. We are so dragged down by our stupour that we never get there. We'd rather zone out when not busy doing something to make a buck. For a whole lifetime, I had to blunt my existence by dealing with people in that stupour. I have seen way too many blank faces when confronted with something foreign to their bailiwick.

I am more and more convinced that the neuro-atypical phenomena is the human race, at the behest of Nature, attempting to take the next step. They are the human race chomping at the bit to attain a new way of life.

It is the shock of the stupour in which no one belongs that befuddles us all and rightly so. No one should any longer be in the stupour that has dogged us for three millennia.

I'm still avoiding the point because the words won't come.

I should probably rename my term for the mysteries of life from Serendipity (you will run across the term in a few of the other books) to Synchronicity or maybe it's a matter of both. I feel, in this lifetime, like I have been beaten to the ground, over and over again. And, I kept getting back up. It is only the stubborn belief in humanity's potential that has kept me going.

The reason I suggest Synchronicity is that it seems like it is all a matter of synchronizing with life. I'll try to think of a better way to explain it but, I think, if you go back and look at some of my descriptions of Serendipity, you will get the gist.

It is like, when one becomes "in tune" with life, everything goes well. That may also tie in with my thoughts on the Trajectory of Life in a big way. Maybe that is the next goal. Getting so in tune with life that everything goes well may be the next big step.

The first big goal is that it is all of humanity that becomes in tune with life.

Sorry, I'm writing this to get it out of my system and on paper. There is a very good chance, I may just let this remain as is. I think I've done enough.

This is not meant to really convince anyone at this point. It is just slapping it down on paper quickly and making it available for perusal and further thought. I guess I could easily say that everything in this chapter is just ruminations that may have potential. If no one has the desire that I do something with it, I don't either. Not anymore. If the human race is really that witless, it's time to give up. Yes, I know how many times I've said that before. At some point, there is an easy exit. The lack of caring displayed by every other member of the human race may just be enough to sweep me there.

Then, again, it is getting interesting once more. I am just so tired of wracking my brain when a concerted effort would make it so much easier.

In some ways, it's so apparent now. We run around seeking pleasure and fulfillment and never fulfilling either, while the pleasure and fulfillment we are seeking is right in front of us. I think I have to go now.

Thank you for reading this book

whickwithy@gmail.com

I just thought it would be nice to reiterate the reason I use this photo. Considering I have spent the last twelve years attempting to form my knowledge and awareness into something that can convey all of the nonsense that we endure and how we finally become human, there has been a whole lot of snarling. That was preceded by an additional forty years to assemble that knowledge and awareness. I have snarled a lot due to the effort, the time gone, and the fact that no one else has been able to get the big picture or even engage in the slightest way.

I hope this does it. Otherwise, it's going to take another lifetime.

I didn't get it easily. The forty years before that, while I was just wondering what is wrong with the human race, weren't so bad. It's been the last twelve years that have been painful.

Men need to fully join the human race.

Oh, by the way, I've been writing down crazy thoughts to ponder them for decades. It's what I do. It just finally came to the point where some of those crazy thoughts started converging on something worth saying. Many of the thoughts, like the fact that the best way to prevent dental damage is to brush your *mouth* (e.g. not just your teeth and especially your *tongue*) with hydrogen peroxide. It seems important to me but not worth the bother of spending a lot of time explaining to the dull-witted, preprogrammed animal. People reject new ideas way too easily and I had no interest in explaining such simple issues in an exhaustive manner when more important issues were at hand. Like preventing cancer without the help of doctors. Like repairing my damaged body without cuts, fusions, and poppycock from doctors.

When people didn't comprehend so many subjects (that have since proved true), I just moved on. It was not as important as what the hell is wrong with humanity. It didn't matter if humanity did not become sane.

While I took attaining our sanity seriously and discovered the key more than a dozen years ago, it was a whole different matter to put it into words that were not influenced by all of the bizarre concepts that our prehuman existence has developed for more than three millennia.

I begin to wonder what would happen if my sentience had not been encumbered by the overwhelming desire to know what the hell is the matter with humanity (wthitmwh).

What would have happened if I had been free to pursue music? Poetry? Any art? Math? Physics? My guess is that my pursuit would have focused on music and lyrics. It seems the second most intriguing mystery since wthitmwh. There's just something about music and how it plays on the emotions.

I don't mean I want to explore all of the technicalities that might be involved. I'm not sure they matter. Like the one I was just reading concerning the effect of rhythmic beats on the psyche. It is now known to have admirable effects on the psyche. It's kind of interesting. Is it that the regular beat gives a rhythm to time? The repetitive score gives almost a feeling of precognition, especially a song I know well. Like a sense of deja vu. Okay, I guess I do want to explore the technicalities.

What I really want to explore is music's mysteries. I was just a bit busy, otherwise, in this life.

Trajectory of life

I want to conclude this book with something I mentioned somewhere along the line. The trajectory of life. Not human life but all of life.

Up until this point in the evolution of life on this planet, I think it suffices to say that the trajectory of life was increased complexity. It started single cell and grew in complexity to us.

I think that view changes radically if one thinks deeply about this revelation regarding all of our trouble and its loving coitus resolution.

At this point, the game changed. It became about consciousness and conscious evolution. It became about understanding.

Nature, if one wishes to personify or animate the background concept of life and its progression, seems to be directed at a truly magnificent goal. I do not believe the goal is love. That is just another necessary tool that Nature has provided to continue progress towards whatever its final goal really is. I do not mean to personify Nature into a conscious entity. But, somehow, Nature seems directed at a goal. Now that it goes beyond just complexity and genes, it just seems that Nature has a purpose, not just making things more complicated. I can't even guess at Nature's long term goal, though there are hints available.

I also sense that a couple of hundred more years may get us breathtakingly closer to that goal.

We are now approaching a transformation from a mudbug to a butterfly. There will be a lot to learn. I believe a lot of it will be revealed in the pursuit of music and rhoetry.

Back to Nature

I stumbled onto a phrase that clicked with what I've been saying about Nature and my own evolving relationship with Nature and its implications for humanity.

"Nature abhors a vacuum". I think I would change that common phrase to "The Trajectory of Nature abhors a vacuum".

This is what I do. When a phrase chimes with another catalogued item, I store it away and keep the link. I set it in my mind's catalog. I doubt I will ever get a good handle on the Trajectory of Nature in this lifetime. Unlike this whole series, I'm not expecting an answer. One day someone will answer the collected questions in a coherent manner.

I doubt you will be able to make sense of the idea that The Trajectory of Nature abhors a vacuum. I have just the slightest sense of it. It is profound but there's no reason to get into it.

Until humanity can figure out how to put away its insanity, it won't mean a thing to anyone. Once humanity is sane, it will begin to make sense. No point, really, in getting into it here.

- This book is going to do with very little editing for a couple of reasons. One is that I think I finally hit a stride on writing prose. It should be mostly coherent on the first draft. Also, I'm tired. I've been at this so mind-bogglingly long.

I haven't much patience left. I know that it is just a matter of circumstances. I know that it is only the matter of the big picture, which no one seems to have ever considered. But, still, it has been an agony. It hurts to think that humanity is so utterly confused that it can't see the light when the door is opened wide.

When do I say quits? I would like it to be when I have finally convey a picture that anyone can comprehend. When do I decide it's not going to happen or I haven't the strength to carry on? I'm pretty much there. I've only gotten this far because I believe in the saying you can't keep a good man down. I started out bent, physically, emotionally, and mentally. I learned to stand up erect in every way. Now, it's time to lie back down.

If there is one area that I would like to clean up it is Details. It's just that it is such a herculean effort to do so at an age when I don't have the enthusiasm.

It's all there. As I've said often, it is easy once we get over all of our delusions. More exactly, we won't get there until we get over our delusions. Once we do, the rest should be amenable to other minds. Articulating it in a more coherent manner should be duck soup, once the barriers are down. So, I concentrated on lifting the veil.

Besides, as I've also often repeated. The man's success at loving coitus will become natural once we accept it is possible with no need for any of these books.

I have to admit I was right in something else I said. There was nothing more to convey after book *Ten*. This book is not so much about conveying anything new, though new perspectives keep cropping up. It's just a matter of wording it in a form that anyone can understand. Now, it is up to some one or more to see their own way through with the help of those words.

I'm not expecting success. It's funny. I should feel utterly bitter but I don't. Bittersweet is all there is. I did something incredible. It was surely better than the monstrous lie that everyone accepts. So, no, I can't feel bad at all. About any of it.

I think I finally get why it is so difficult to convey all of this. It hits at too many levels. Worse yet, it is difficult to say precisely what one means to convey, amidst the abiding humanity-wide delusions, when engaging this subject matter. The fault is not in the words but in the delusions.

When our existence is filled with gibberish because we are ashamed of an act that we engage in regularly, it becomes that much more difficult to explain what everyone is hiding from. No one can raise their heads and take a look. When addressing the issue of shame, it becomes *almost* impossible.

I can only hope I succeeded. I won't be trying again, unless a miracle or another lifetime occurs.

It continues to blow my mind how this has all progressed. I've mentioned already a lot of reasons why it blows my mind. I have another. The timing of coincident events is incredible.

While I got the slightest taste of success at coitus at a very advanced age, the fires began to burn low. I could not do what is my usual proclivity: face a problem head on. At the time I achieved success, I had not sussed out all that there is to know about the situation.

As the fires burned lower and lower (for reasons I'm not going to get into), the only way I continued to explore was because I *had* to approach it from a technical perspective. I had to learn to analyze the conditions and results rather than live them. This was key. I'm not sure I would have gotten there if the fires had not burned low. In fact, the whole experience of seventy years followed that route. Everything revealed itself as it became too late for me to do anything about it on a personal level. I could only attempt to convey it to others for the sake of the sanity of humankind.

You'll see the progression in my understanding of the situation through the eleven books, though there may be some anachronistic elements since I rewrote a lot in the preceding books as I mosied along the way.

All of the nuances of why and how a man can achieve loving coitus was a long trail littered with the misconceptions we have held onto for ages. We stunted our existence because we were convinced loving coitus was too much, too difficult, for humanity. We were woefully wrong.

Nothing works right for a sentient race as long as sex is out of skew. If you haven't noticed, sex is way out of skew. Our perceptions regarding heterosexual intimacies are warped. Our whole sexual landscape is warped. Women should be having orgasms during coitus.

Maybe some opt out but it has to become an option for everyone, not a predetermined failure of coitus that isn't even acknowledged.

As I age, to like really old age, I realize my attitude is in a position to understand the woman's point of view. The unrelenting male urge to sexual release (orgasm in impolite society) has eased off and I can just live.

There's something to say for it. Let me be clear, though, once again. It is not that unrelenting urge that destroys men. It is the unrelenting urge combined with utter failure to make something human of it all.

I am really hitting some lows, right now. I think there are a lot of reasons. My life has not been lived, it has been sacrificed. It is another deeply held belief of mine that one does not want any praise for something like this. It's more complicated than that. It is that no single person should be attached to the concept. I am disgusted that I had to push so hard to gain any awareness of the subject. That is the fundamental reason I have maintained my anonymity.

I think there is a lesson there that I have been avoiding. I think the lesson is that humanity is just not ready. It makes me sad.

I have never been closer to the tip of the razor's edge. It has been a very confusing life. It staggers me to realize that all of my writings were love letters to some extent.

This life can never, of course, become only a thoughtful life for anyone. It is, after all, a physical life. But, it sure could use a ton more individual thought and less herd reaction.

That is only true in a contemplation of life sense for me. For me, the physical side of it will never be complete now. Especially complete in the manner that a woman takes so casually. The fulfillment of a lover in the best way possible.

I don't know what to do with that. It's a Catch-44 for me. Entertainment of the mind, once we are fully human, will not be enough but thinking will also be celebrated rather than avoided, finally. I would be starting from square one in more ways than you can imagine.

Entertainment of the mind is not drowning one's brain in damaging substances like alcohol, nicotine or any substance in excess or tv shows. But, really, really celebrating life.

Sigh. Do you get it yet? We nix the celebration of life because the most perfect way in which to celebrate life has been nipped in the bud since animals ever existed. We have not made life human. We just followed the most obvious trail that the animal presented, like a herd of animals.

It is not truly celebrated when the man has to take a pill. It's just another version of an animal's solution.

The human sees that unassisted, successful, loving coitus is within its reach. Let me be clear, once again, for a last time. The human *race* must comprehend this. Not a few individuals. It has to become part of the global consciousness.

I don't think it's going to be that difficult. But, come what may, we have to take the step. We have to face the fact, openly, with open discussion, that the most natural form of the act of love has, so far, failed. What do we do about it?

My knowledge and understanding of the dilemma is in 'Details'. My knowledge and understanding of the complete conundrum of our missing humanity is littered through eleven books and quite a few other writings.

- It has taken so long to realize the truth because we placed ourselves in a stupour in order to avoid the subject of what is wrong with humanity because each generation failed to overcome the problem. At puberty, their minds begin to shut down.

We have avoided the mirror ever since it became clear that love was missing in its most essential form. Because of embarrassment and shame, we cut off sentient thought. We essentially quit thinking long ago, when it came to anything we saw in the mirror.

We couldn't understand. We were lousy at sex. Only one gender was responsible for the failure and there didn't seem to be a thing they could do about it.

Round robin. Men couldn't do anything about it because we couldn't spend a moment thinking on the subject. We couldn't spend a moment thinking about it because we were convinced we couldn't do anything about it. The foundations of our faulty perceptions kept hitting us in the face any time we tried to think. Reminds me of Hitchhikers Guide To The Universe.

It is incredible, in retrospect, that we could never get beyond the concept that there remains some time limit on the act of coitus, for a sentient race, other than exhaustion or full satisfaction.

Don't you find it curious that we have been able to use the gifts that Nature provides to a sentient race to rain down destruction on all and sundry and, yet, we have not figured out how to use those gifts to fulfill unassisted loving coitus? We won't be human until we have conquered the animal in us. It starts with conquering unassisted loving coitus. Until then, we have conquered nothing of importance.

- Why is it that no one seems to be able to see the animal's reign in all we do? Or, is humanity naive enough to believe this is the best we can do?

- Can no one see the repetitive nature of our history? Two aspects of the animal drive us as long as we remain a distorted version of an animal and never attain our true sentient state. Fear and 'greed'. I put greed in quotes because, in the sense of survival, one might call refer to is as a 'hunger'. Humanity's un-satiated hunger is for love. Not all of the substitutes that we accept in its absence can make up for its absence.

It goes in cycles. As the greed (or hunger) builds within a culture, any remnants of love are cast off. Any remnants of our humanity atrophy. Then comes the wars and killing on tremendous scale.

After humanity has rained down enough destruction, the fear of just how awful humanity can be begins to dawn for a little while. We step lightly for a few decades, while the fear grips us. The horror of our behaviour begins to wear off as three generations pass. It becomes a second-hand experience. Then, we are at it again.

It will never go away until we learn to love in its most perfected form. All of the substitutes will never get us there. That doesn't mean the substitutes don't have their place. It just means that they are not enough on their own.

If our sentience could not overcome the failure, that would be different. We would have to find another way. The biggest part of which is being open to the dilemma instead of sweeping it under the rug.

I will never believe that a highly sophisticated, intelligent race that is so desperate for love can fail. Humanity has been provided by Nature with the tools to overcome the failure of *unassisted* loving coitus that an animal must endure. I stress unassisted because pills are a stupid animal's resolution. It is not flexing our sentient capabilities.

I used rhoetry to remove the subconscious from the equation.

Maybe the most frustrating aspect of this task I took on is that I leave everyone dumbfounded. It's that big of a leap. It was the only way to clear the flotsam from our lives.

Ah, well, I'm about done. I hope I get through.

I think I will make a prediction, even though I despise the idea of prophetic utterings. It is never anything more than extrapolations (or pure bullshit).

It just makes sense to me. Once we become human in every way, playing and creating music will be one of the ultimate pursuits. I hope most everyone takes part. That's not a prediction. Just a hope.

Music is both a skill and the most incredible form of creativity. It is used to explore everything important on the spiritual side of a human, sentient existence. It hints at so much.

Love does not do away with the material side of existence. We, of course, will need to provide for the material side of life but that is not where the orientation of a sentient race resides. It will be simple for a sane, sentient race to provide for all of its constituents.

Altogether, it is going to be the greatest reorientation ever seen on Earth. An animal that has attained a sentient state fully.

As I've said before, it will not be a revolution. It will not turn life upside down, like revolutions do. It will start as just a change in tone as couples finally become content with their relationships. It radiates outward from there.

We will move on toward more important efforts. The first effort, of course, will be to right our course.

We can make the current structure work to some extent without change. As I've said often, the organization of humankind is not the most severe problem. The most severe problem is humankind itself not realizing it is far different from the animal due to a single act that means everything in that it initiates the fullest expression of love.

That doesn't mean the structures of our life won't change. It just won't change at the madcap pace that a bewildered animal takes because it is out of its depth.

Since we won't be having sex just as an excuse to have babies, we can control our propagation to a much greater degree. The population can ebb and flow as humanity and the times require. Not by decree but through the sense of a sentient race.

There is this mad belief by prehumans that growth is all there is. If we are not expanding like mad, we believe we have failed. I am not saying that growth is bad. I am not saying anything about the necessity of growth. I haven't a clue but I am certain growth is not the be-all to end-all. I am not even certain that any issues with providing for all of humanity stem from too much population. But, I am certain that a sane, emotionally stable, rational, loving race of sentient beings will figure it out.

All we have ever tried to do for the last three millennia is distract ourselves from the debacle, not ever resolve it.

www.ingramcontent.com/pod-product-compliance
Lightning Source LLC
La Vergne TN
LVHW020658100826
845148LV00012B/2561

* 9 7 8 1 7 3 4 8 2 2 1 8 2 *